STARTING AN ONLINE BUSINESS AND INTERNET MARKETING 2021

Guide to Setting up an E-Commerce Website, SEO, and Digital Marketing Strategies.

S. K. HOLDER

CONTENTS

Introduction

What is the Book About?

- How to set up an e-Commerce website
- Website configuration and management for Google search engine optimization (SEO).
- Driving more traffic through social media and other digital marketing techniques.
- Measuring performance with Google Analytics
- Running pay-per-click advertising campaigns.
- E-Commerce business models, including dropshipping and the sale of digital products.
- Passive income ideas, such as affiliate marketing and Google AdSense.
- The elements of good web design.

Who is the Book for?

This book is intended for small businesses, start-ups and individual entrepreneurs who want to manage their own online business effectively for Google search engine optimization, to familiarize themselves with common content management system (CMS) features, track their business metrics, and manage their digital marketing and pay-per-click campaigns.

What Topics are Covered in this Book and Where Should I Start?

The topics in this book involve managing your website on the client - that is from the administration dashboard of your content management system (CMS). It also offers advice for small changes you might want to make to the code files. You will learn to write the sort of content that generates shares and follows, how to work with influencers, grow your brand, retain your followers, write great captions and titles, integrate your social media accounts with your blog, understand the psychology that drives online engagement, and much more.

In addition, you will learn about some of the more popular e-commerce business models, as well as social media marketing, managing pay-per-click (PPC) advertising campaigns with Google Ads and Facebook.

In terms of SEO, we will focus on optimizing for Google's search engine. We will also discuss how to set up and add products to an online shop and cover some common technical issues.

You will often hear digital marketing specialists say that there is no proven method for online success.

It is easy to get caught in a frenzy of trying every single marketing strategy out there, in the hope that it will catapult your business to instant success.

What often happens is that you cannot see the results of your digital labor or anyone else's because you do not know enough about what's under the hood, or how to track your website's performance. As a result, you waste time and money.

This is your business. Do not be ignorant. You will need to teach yourself about the digital landscape before launching any online business. I am not saying you need a diploma, but you should understand the fundamentals.

———

Business Models

Types of E-Commerce business models
There are four main e-commerce business models:
- Print-on-demand
- White Label manufacturing
- Drop shipping
- Wholesale

Print on Demand model
Print-on-demand (POD) can include print books, artwork, mugs, t-shirts, hoodies, phone cases, towels, and more. Some of the top POD providers are Red Bubble, TeeSpring, Shopify, Amazon Merch, Printify, and Zazzle.

White Label manufacturing
If you have created a product, and want to sell it to another individual or business, and take none of the credit, then you can opt for white label manufacturing. The company or person who you sell your product to will rebrand it under their own name.

Dropshipping model
With dropshipping, you host a website with products using a dropship merchant, who will ship the products directly to your customers.

Wholesalers
If you are sourcing products from wholesalers,

go to a wholesaler directory, e.g. <u>salehoo</u>. You can buy wholesale products from China's e-commerce companies: <u>Alibaba</u> or <u>DHgate</u>.

Passive income
You should also seek to make passive income from your business. Passive income is the additional revenue you can make, on the back of your e-commerce site, that will continue to bring in income long after the initial set up. Passive income streams can include:

- <u>Creating a digital product,</u> e.g. an eBook
- <u>Affiliate marketing</u>
- Creating an app
- Membership subscription
- <u>Google AdSense</u>
- Renting advertising space

These passive income streams should be anchored to your e-commerce website.

Advertising model
If you are doing affiliate marketing, you can use an advertising business model to target a list of email subscribers, who you will then send to your affiliate links.

What are Solo ads?
High ticket programs
High ticket programs are usually associated with sales starting from $1000 and can go up to $25,000 or more. The products can be anything

from digital, coaching, or consultation products that provide high-value training that satisfies a consumer need. This could be a quality eBook, a webinar series, or a training course hosted on a platform like Udemy.

What is Dropshipping?
Dropshipping is when a third-party, i.e. a supplier delivers items to your customer on your behalf.

When a customer buys something from your website, you will access your dropshipping account and place the order, providing the customer's delivery address in place of your own.

For example, a customer buys a headphone set on your website. You sell it at the R.R.P. of $39.99. You will then log in to your dropship suppliers account and buy the item for $30.00 wholesale price (with dropship admin fees, postage costs and VAT applied) you will make a profit of $9.99.

Advantages of Dropshipping

- You do not need to hold stock. This is ideal if you are operating an e-commerce store out of your home.
- You can process orders faster, leaving

time for you to focus on sourcing new products and marketing.
- You can minimize administrative and postage costs.
- You do not have to worry about product images as your dropshipper will supply these.

Disadvantages of Dropshipping

- Your profit margins may be low due to administrative charges applied to your dropshipping account. This means that you are more likely to see a higher return on investment than if you opt for a standard wholesaler account.
- You may find that your dropship supplier is your biggest competition. Many dropship providers have their own website. Often long established, they will have a higher Google rank and offer discounts of which you may not be able to compete.
- Your dropship supplier may restrict where you can sell items. For example, they may stipulate that you cannot sell their products on eBay or Amazon.
- Dropship suppliers will not handle your return items. If, for whatever reason, the customer does not want the item, you will need to set up a business parcel return service or find an alternative

address for customers to return unwanted items. You will then have to pick them up from this address or pay extra to have the items delivered to your home address. It is then up to you to try to sell the unwanted items. Rarely, will your dropship suppliers buy the items back from you.

- You do not have control over order fulfilment and timely deliveries. Dropshipped orders can take longer to reach your customers'. Remember that your dropship suppliers are dealing with hundreds or thousands of other account-holders like yourself. There is a wait, and you may find the item is out of stock by the time you place the order. This delay will reflect badly on your business and you can lose customers as a result.
- The market is saturated with e-commerce sites offering the same products from popular dropshipping suppliers. Unless you have something different to offer, you will not see a high return.

Dropshipping Tips

- Do not copy and paste product descriptions from your dropship suppliers' website. This will have a negative impact on your search engine

rank.
- Do not issue a refund to the customer until you have confirmation from the postal returns service that they have received the item.
- Provide your own invoice to the dropshipper which they can include with your customers' orders. This will ensure that the customer knows the item came from your website and not your dropship suppliers.
- Go for high-value items for a good return on investment.
- Dropshipping is better for smaller and medium size businesses.
- Do your research. Many dropshipping e-commerce sites are spawned from a single dropship provider, all of which are selling the same products. If you want to succeed in dropshipping, you need to offer something different from the competition.

Affiliate Programs

If done the right way, your online business can benefit from affiliate programs. To maximize a ROI (return on investment), it helps if you have a large social media following and or/email list.

A popular affiliate program is **Amazon Affiliates**. It is easy to set up. However, the commission is low – as little as 4% – as oppose to other companies who can pay 50% or more.

ClickBank is a popular choice for digital products.

The most effective way to make money through an affiliate program is to promote it, which can be time-consuming. If you have the budget, you can use an affiliate broker, such as Affiliate by Conversant (formerly Commission Junction) or TradeDoubler.com to manage your affiliates for you.

Affiliate Marketing Steps

Starting affiliate marketing involves several steps:

Step 1: Decide what you want to promote. It should be something you understand and are passionate about.

Step 2: Research and compile a list of affiliate merchants. Check out the merchant's websites. What's the commission rate? Do they offer reoccurring commissions? Do they provide quality promotional materials? What is the overall competitiveness?

Step 3: Decide where you are going to promote your affiliates. To do this you will need a landing page. You can sign up for a single landing page with an online sales funnel builder service, e.g. clickfunnels. Alternatively, you can create your own website. WordPress is a good option because it has lots of support plugins for affiliate marketers. You can also promote affiliates on social media platforms using paid ads.

Step 4: Decide how to promote your affiliates. The most effective way to promote affiliates is through lead capture. You create a single landing page with a sign-up form. Ask the visitor to sign up to your mailing list. (You can offer a free eBook in return for their sign up). Once they have signed up, you can send them your affiliate link using an autoresponder email. Once on your email list, you can send follow up emails and other offers containing your affiliate links.

Tips for Promoting Affiliates

- Write an article about the affiliate product in your blog or news column. I suggest you try the product, then you can write a pros and cons review, preferably with a comparison product. You can also create videos and add images of yourself trying out the product.
- Do not promote an affiliate whose page does not convert. If the affiliate isn't getting visitors to their site, and the

product is poor or overpriced, you will be wasting your time.

- You need to know your audience and do your research. You can make serious money from affiliates if you are prepared to pay to promote them, usually through pay-per-click advertising.
- Promote your affiliates through social media, podcasts, webinars, and your email list.
- Read Google's Console pages regarding duplicate content to ensure that you do not fall foul to Google's Panda algorithm, which has a negative impact on the classic link-placing affiliate model.
- Promote by guest posting on blogs and forums.
- Do a product giveaway or contest.
- Measure your affiliate performance using analytic tools.
- Promote select quality products.
- Choose more than one affiliate program.

Top Affiliate Programs

- A popular affiliate program is <u>Amazon Affiliates</u>. It's easy to set up. However, the commission is low – as little as 4% – as oppose to other companies who can pay 50% or more. To make serious

money, you would need to promote high-ticket items.
- ClickBank is a popular choice for digital products.
- JVZoo is a good place to start, if you're a beginner. It offers a good user experience. On average, you can earn 50% per sale.
- Conversant (formerly Commission Junction). This is a large network of companies offering affiliates. Once you've signed up, you will need to make individual applications to the companies whose products or services you want to promote.
- You can also search for individual companies offering affiliates. This will be displayed on their website.

Other Affiliate Business Models

- You can start your own affiliate program to encourage others to promote your business. You can pay them a commission for every sale or lead they bring you.
- You can open a gift store that will send your visitors on to the websites of your affiliates.

Selling Digital Products

Your CMS should facilitate the sale of downloadable/virtual products. With zero overheads and high profit margins, you should consider selling downloadable products that are relevant to your business. eBooks are becoming increasingly popular.

There are many platforms for you to publish eBooks. Amazon is the most popular because it drives the highest traffic in comparison with other online booksellers.

In the back of your eBook, provide a link to your website. You should also advertise your eBook on your website.

You can sell your eBook for as little as $0.99. You will need to join Amazon KDP. Check their website for details.

eBooks are not the only digital products that sell well. You can also sell royalty free digital products, such as videos, audio narrative, music, templates, graphics, photos, and web apps.

The advantage of having a digital product is that you need only create or purchase one version. As you do not have to hold physical stock, you do not have to worry about postage and shipping costs.

You can find digital products to sell with "resell rights" online, or better still create your own unique product to cut out the competition.

If you want to sell different types of digital products on one website, you will make more money from a membership model than selling the digital products individually. Ask members to sign up to unlock access to your products depending on the membership level you set, i.e. bronze, gold, platinum.

Tips for Selling Downloadable Products

- Consider selling the downloadable material in a bundle rather than standalone.
- Upload multiple products in a zip file.
- Do not forget to add a section in your website's footer explaining how and where the customer can download their product after purchase.
- Consider offering some free digital products to retain existing customers and bring in new ones.

A Quick Checkout

Consumers want a quick checkout for digital products. If you are unable to offer this, you will get little or no sales. Select a CMS that allows buyers to bypass the shipping information and registration process because, while many popular content management systems cater for the sale of downloadable products, buyers are still required to provide their shipping address and, in some cases, register for an account. Virtual products do not require a physical billing address, they require, at most, an email address.

Ideally, you will want to use a CMS with a digital eStore plugin or extension.

Legal Requirements for the Sale of Digital Products

If the product is faulty, you must give the customer 30 days to notify you of this. You must offer a replacement or refund. Place this information in the **Shipping and Returns** section of your website.

Storage Space

Some content management systems require additional configuration to accommodate file sizes larger than 20 MB. Video files are typically more than 100 MB. Therefore, do not opt for a lower subscription plan, if you intend to sell more than just eBooks.

Add the file size in your product description

If you are selling software, the consumer needs to know they have the space on their hard drive to complete the download. Example:

How to make money online (PDF | 360 KB)

How to increase the file size upload in a cPanel

You may get a message stating that your file is too large to upload.

If you are using a cPanel, click on "Service Configuration" where you should see the **"PHP Configuration Editor"**.

Change the "upload_max_filesize" to the file size you require.

For example, if you have an **upload_max_filesize=20 MB**, you can increase it to **upload_max_filesize = 250 MB**

Alternatively, you can change the upload_max_filesize by accessing the **File Manage**r code files. If you are using WordPress, you will find the upload_max_filesize in the "File Uploads" section. Do not forget to save your changes.

———

Google AdSense

You can make passive income with Google AdSense. This involves placing other people's ads on your website to generate revenue. You will get paid each time someone clicks on one of the Google ads supplied on your website. You need to set up a Google AdSense account.

Google will then provide you with some JavaScript code to add to the sections of your website where you want the ads displayed.

You can decide which types of ads you want to display. The popular choice is a combination of text and display ads. The reality is you would need to get an average of 10,000 visitors to your website per day, to earn around £7.50/ $10.00.

Google AdSense will send you a pin that you will need to confirm for the ads to run. They will review your website before approval. You will also need to ensure that you are posting original and not duplicate content on your website.

If you want to make passive income from AdSense, then you will need to use the top competitive keywords in your chosen niche. Use high-paying keywords from the Google Keyword Planner found under the "Tools" or spanner icon of your Google Ads account.

Add AdSense ads to the top pages of your website not to the bottom.

As of April 2017, you can no longer run Google AdSense ads on your YouTube channel if you have under 10,000 views. Video traffic is big business. If you build your YouTube channel by regularly posting videos that people want to watch, you can generate this number of views and make a good income from AdSense advertising.

Note that it is not good practice to use AdSense for e-commerce because the ads can cause visitors navigate away from your website.

Understanding Sales Funnels

These days, you cannot simply put a website on the internet and expect the money to start rolling in. With over 2 million pieces of content uploaded to the internet daily, the competition is tough.

You will need to create a filtration system. This is known as a sales funnel. A funnel is wider at the top and narrower at the bottom. Imagine you are getting 10,000 visitors to your site, but only 100 of those result in a conversion. You must find a way of filtering out those who are not interested in your products.

For a sales funnel to work, you need to show that your product adds value by solving a problem. You need to build trust, and show that you are offering something that your competitors are not.

Think about the benefits of your product and the problem it solves. Remember that your product is the solution. Think about the way you shop online as a customer and what prompts you to make a purchase.

What Does a Sales Funnel Consist of?

A **content funnel** and a **conversion funnel**.

A **content funnel** will consist of your website pages, articles and blogs. In terms of blogs and articles, the content should be visually appealing and tied to some emotional trigger: excitement, joy, relief, etc. Question-based content and list-based content is easier for people to digest because people tend to scan for information on the web rather than read word-for-word.

Your **conversion funnel** is your call-to-action, e.g. the checkout process or an email capture page.

If you are selling products your content funnel will be the product page. Buyer prompts will be an attention-grabbing headline, the description, product images, starred-reviews, etc.

How do you Build Trust?

Through credibility demonstrated by reviews, testimonials, product comparisons.

How do you Know if your Sales Funnel is Working?

For a start, you will be making a profit. Analyze the behavior flow in Google Analytics to see how visitors move through your site. Find out which route leads to a sale and recreate similar product pages. You can also do split variation testing, by creating two different product pages and testing which one leads to a conversion.

———

Domain Names

Choosing a Domain Name

Choose a unique domain name, not one that is similar to your competition. Brand names tend to rank higher than domain names that are based on keyword search terms.

Choose a domain name that is easy to remember and that does not include hyphens or numbers. I advise you to purchase a .com domain name extension, and a domain name extension, for your own country, if you live outside the USA.

How to Link a Domain to a Hosting Provider Service

If you live in the United Kingdom and plan to ship within the UK, buy a co.uk domain name. You may later decide that you want to sell internationally and will want to set up a .com website as well. Purchase both domain name extensions and then you will always have the option to grow your online store.

A few of the best places to buy a domain name are godaddy.com, namecheap.com, and 123-reg.co.uk.

Once you have brought your domain name and

installed your CMS, you will need to access your domain name account and connect it to the hosting provider's server from there. If your server is not hooked up to your domain name, you will not be able to see your website when you type the website address into your web browser.

Your hosting provider will give you your DNS (Domain Name Server) information.

Your domain name server, set up information will usually consist of two server addresses, which will look something like this:

XX1.Servername.com
XX2.Servername.com

Add this information to the fields provided in your domain name account dashboard. This is the website from which you brought the domain name, not your CMS admin dashboard.

———

Content Management Systems and Shopping Cart Solutions

What is a Content Management System?

A content management system (CMS) is an application that allows you to produce and modify digital content. A CMS provides a great many add-ons in the form of widgets and plugins to alter and extend its functionality.

Widgets are small applications that you can add to your website to extend its functionality without having to go into the code files to make changes. An example of a widget is a Nivo Slider, which allows you to add sliding images with links to the front page of your website. You may also have a Google Analytics widget on your website to place your tracking code, or HTML widgets to add text or images to areas on your page.

Plugins or add-ons, add a specific feature to your website. There are literally hundreds of available website plugins. Your CMS will come with some pre-installed plugins, e.g. promotional feeds, payment methods, shipping rate computation packages, Facebook Connect authentication, and tax providers, etc.

Managing your CMS may be daunting at first and certainly time-consuming. I would advise you to write a list of all the features on your CMS dashboard and check them off as you complete them.

Self-hosting solutions are more flexible because you can make changes to the code and script files. While self-hosting solutions are cheaper than hosted solutions, you may find it time-consuming to get the support you need for installation, set up and site administration.

WooCommerce is an e-commerce plugin for WordPress which means it is easily customizable. Other self-hosting options include Drupal, ZenCart, Joomla, and Magento. (While extremely flexible, Magento is more suitable for medium to large businesses).

Shopify and BigCommerce are two of the best e-commerce hosted-solutions. You can sell unlimited products on their website. Although, you will not have access to the code files, they are easy to install and highly customizable. The minimum subscription for their all-features online store costs around $29.99/£23.00 per month.

Volusion is another hosted-solution with a starting price of around $29.99/£23.00. Volusion is good for selling digital products. You could also try Payhip, which offers a free option, if you have 100 digital products or less to sell.

Important Note: Always update your CMS to the latest version. Do this without delay or you will experience technical issues and your website will open to cyber-attacks.

———

Hosting Service Providers

A hosting service provider will rent out a space on their server for you to run your website. You can normally add a minimum of two websites from your virtual web hosting dashboard for only a few dollars/pounds a month.

Look for a SSD (Solid State Driver) hosting provider. SSD drives load 20 times faster than the traditional turbo drives, which means your website pages will load quicker.

Thoroughly research web hosting service providers before committing. Look for online reviews and check "Uptime" scores. Good hosting providers should offer 24-hour technical support, server reliability, easy to use hosting panels, email account hosting, daily site backups, unlimited bandwidth and unlimited domains, at no extra cost. Some hosting providers even offer free domain names and website builders.

It is possible to install and manage your own website with no web development or programming experience. However, do not expect your hosting providers to come to your rescue every time you get stuck with website configuration.

Do not forget you are renting a space from them. Let me give you an analogy. If you are renting a space in the car park, you would not contact the car park owner every time you had a problem with your car. You would go to a mechanic, unless the problem with your car was caused by someone or something within the car park.

By managing your control panel, you have become your own website host provider. This is known as **self-hosting.**

cPanels for Self-Hosting

A cPanel is a virtual web hosting account provided by your hosting service provider. The panel itself, or dashboard if you like, enables you to configure and manage your website and set up your email accounts. A premium cPanel comes complete with a wide selection of content management systems that you can easily install for free. Each CMS has demos, examples and reviews which you can view in your cPanel, or you can visit the CMS provider's website for more information.

cPanel web hosting accounts can cost as little as $4.00/£3.00 per month for just two websites.

You can also find plenty of cPanel help forums and relevant video tutorials on YouTube.

Note, you are responsible for setting up and managing your CMS, not the hosting provider. You should only contact them if you are having problems with the cPanel dashboard and issues with the server.

Try hostinguk.net or a2hosting.com for cPanel self-hosting.

Code and Script Files

Your domain name code and script files are kept in the **File Manager** of your hosting provider account and should be visible on your hosting provider admin dashboard.

If you have a quality CMS, you will seldom need to amend the files, if at all. And if you do need to make any amendments, they will normally be in the HTML scripts which relate to the way the website looks and not the way it functions.

If you feel confident that you can make changes and you have some experience in web development and/or programming, I suggest you copy and paste the original file information to a word document and save it to your computer, that way you will not lose the original settings if you make a mistake.

Reasons for Accessing your File Manager

- To make changes to the CSS files, e.g. the footer, theme, header, etc.
- To add plugins or widgets
- To upload images
- To upload JavaScript files, e.g. EU cookie warning scripts, Google js. tracking code
- To manually upload a favicon

———

Website Design Themes

To create the ultimate shopping experience for your visitors, you need to offer them the virtual equivalent of a physical shop. Think about your storefront. What colors would you paint it? What fonts would you choose for your price tags and the sign above the door?

- Web design should be consistent across all pages in terms of fonts, size, graphics, and colors.
- Except for red, "buy" buttons can be in any color.
- Do not litter your website with annoying pop-ups. This can result in visitors leaving your site.
- Do not use too many colors in your theme. Four is usually sufficient.
- Use "Call to Action" (CTA) links sparingly across your site.
- Include any testimonials, reviews and industry awards.

Choose your theme wisely. More people are buying products from their phones than ever before. I suggest you purchase a mobile responsive template or install it from your CMS. Select your template before getting your logo because it is easier to change the logo than it is to make changes to a theme stylesheet. There is no point in purchasing a green and white theme for your website when you have a purple logo; the colors will clash.

You want your website to look appealing. You may also find that you want to apply your theme color scheme to your business cards and any other promotional products you have to offer.

If you are looking for themes and templates for your website, try themeforest.net.

If you want a unique template, you can employ the services of a digital agency, or find a freelance web designer on websites such as peopleperhour.com, and upwork.com if you simply want to change the color scheme and layout of an existing theme template.

If you are self-hosting your website, you will find your theme folders in your File Manager usually in a folder named "Themes". It will have a ".css" file extension and will be named "style.css".

Cascading stylesheets (CSS) are used to describe the look and format of HTML elements on your website. Your theme folder is likely to contain multiple stylesheets that will apply to different sections of your website. Some web templates are sophisticated enough to allow you to make changes to the colors and fonts from the CMS dashboard, which means that you will not have to access the code files.

———

Your Logo

Your logo is a representation of your business brand. It must be unique, simple and easily recognizable. It should be high-resolution and in a vector format.

Remember, your logo is not just going to be on your website. It will be on your packaging, invoices, business cards, social media platforms, and banners, as well as any promotional merchandise you produce. Therefore, choose your logo carefully because changing it can cost you a lot of time and money.

You should have already settled on the color palette for your website. Your logo should therefore match your web theme.

You can create your own logo using an online generator tool. Just search under the term, "Logo Design Maker". These websites let you select your design from a set of pre-populated images and set your own fonts, colors and layouts. You can build the logo on these sites for free, but will need to pay in order to download the logos for use on your website.

To get your desired logo, play with different images and fonts. Design the logo in several variations and color schemes.

Alternatively, you can design your own logo using royalty-free vector images. Vector images can be edited when opened in editing suites like Photoshop, Adobe Illustrator and InDesign.

You can also pay for a custom logo. Try a freelance service provider like fiverr.com, upwork.com or 99Design.co.uk.

Consider placing your company slogan beneath the logo on your website. This will be your Unique Selling Proposition (USP). For example, "Quality Products at Divine Prices".

How to Manually Resize your Logo

Your CMS usually allocates a fixed size for your logo. If you want to adjust the size of your logo so that it fits the page, you should be able to resize it by accessing your hosting account File Manager and then amending the content-type in the Header section.

Here is the code snippet:

<!DOCTYPE html
<html lang="en-US">
<head profile=
"http://www.yourwebsitename.com/profile">

<img
src="https://yourwebsitename.com/yourwebsitelog
o.png"   width="250"   height="60"   alt="

mywebsitelogo">

```
</head>
</html>
```

How to Add a Favicon to your Website

To add your image logo, so that it appears in the page tab of your website, you can convert the image to a shortcut icon, also known as a favicon, using an online **Favicon Generator Tool**. Size 16px x 16px tends to work best.

How to Manually add a Favicon to your Website

If you cannot upload your favicon from your CMS, you can upload it to the relevant folder in the File Manager of your hosting account dashboard, e.g. cPanel. You may have to upload it to a designated image folder where you upload all your image files, or you may add it to the root directory of your website, i.e. wwwroot

If you have uploaded your favicon to your root directory, find the <head> section in your Header file and add the following HTML code:

```
<!DOCTYPE html

<html lang="en-US">
<head
profile="http://www.yourwebsitename.com/profile"
>
```

```
<link rel="icon" type="image/ico"
href="http://yourwebsitename.com/favicon.ico" />
</head>
</html>
```

———

Website Footers

Here is a list of some information you will want to place in your footer, i.e. at the bottom of your website:

- Categories
- Cookie Policy
- Shipping and Returns
- Links to your social media pages
- Blog
- Contact information
- Terms and Conditions
- Sitemap
- Privacy Notice
- SSL secure website icon
- Payment method images
- A unique description of your website
- Copyright Information
- Accreditation logos

To further enhance your search engine rankings, add a description about your website using a keyword-set that you have not repeated anywhere else on your website. Try not to add links to internal pages of your website in your footer if they are repeated elsewhere. Search engines will penalize you for this and your ranking will go down. For example, do not litter your website with internal links for your contact information, by adding it to the footer, to the top, right and center of the page. In addition, you should never place external links in the footer as they are not good for SEO.

Note: you will normally have to pay a fee to remove the CMS provider name from the footer.

———

Global Settings

Default Page Title

Add a default page title (also known as a title tag) to your whole website. It will show up in the search engine page results. Your title tag should be no more than 70 characters long. If your website name includes relevant keywords you can use this in your page title. You can also use a page title separator, such as a vertical line (|) or a dash (–) to add an additional keyword search term. Where possible use long-tail keywords, not single keywords. For example, you have a website called lovingdresses.com. Your page title could be:

Loving Dresses | Online Dress Boutique UK

A poor page title would look something like this:
Clothes | Dresses

Consumers only search for single keywords if it is a brand name.

Default Meta Keywords

You do not need these. Bing is the only search engine to use meta keywords and that is only to look for spam. If you do want to add them, for your own reference, do not duplicate the keywords in your default meta description. Use your top keywords in the meta description.

Default Meta Description

Your website meta description should be between 255 and 300 characters long. It should be unique. List a few popular selling products and/or brand names in your website description. It is important that your meta description is not simply a list of the products you have for sale. And whatever you do, do not use the same keywords repeatedly.

The purpose of a meta description is to increase the likelihood that a user will click on your site. The first 300 characters is what users see in SERPs. If you do not add a meta description, search engines will display the first 300 characters of text on the page.

I suggest you do some keyword research to find the keywords that are relevant to your business. Try typing variations of your keyword into the Google search box and see which popular search terms Google displays as you start to type, and then scroll to the bottom of the page to see the searches related to that keyword.

———

Category Pages

Before you add products to your website, you will first need to add your product attributes and create your product category pages. For search engines, your category pages are more important than your product pages as they make it easier for search engines to accurately index your site.

Creating Category Pages

Below is an example of a category named Menswear, which consists of two subcategories: shirts and trousers.

Menswear category

Menswear >> Shirts
Menswear >> Trousers

- Your category menu should be added to the top of your page.
- Try to create keyword-specific categories and subcategories.
- Do not make your category names too long or they will not fit in the page menu.
- Do not add too many subcategories. Visitors may become overwhelmed and confused, if you display too many options.
- Add a detailed category description and

include your relevant keywords.
- Add a price range for your category.

If you plan to regularly sell many discounted products, consider having a "sales" category. This is because the terms: cheap and sale are popular consumer keywords.

Remember that your category pages are more important to search engines than your product pages, so plan them carefully.

Manufacturers/Brand Information
Complete this in full. You can boost sales by optimizing these pages. Some consumers will search for products by manufacturer or brand name. It may be the one keyword search term they use to land on your website. These consumers are often searching for reliability and quality. Add the manufacturer/brand logo to your manufacturer pages.

Price Range Field
Complete the price range field if you have one. The price range should be realistic for the manufacturer's price range.

For example:

-60;60-150;150-;

Here, I am allowing the consumer to choose between Brett and Mann products of less than $60, between $60.00 and $150.00, or more than $150.00.

The manufacturer description should be at least 150 characters of your own words and should sound as natural as possible. The main keyword here is the brand name, "Brett and Mann". Shoppers may expand their search term on this keyword to "Brett and Mann Clothes" or "Clothing by Brett and Mann".

For example:

This clothing company was founded by John Brett and Alan Mann in 1956. They make quality silk clothing for men, including ties, jumpers and jackets.

Your meta title should be brand specific. For example:
Brett and Mann | Men's Silk Clothing

The above example is fine if Brett and Mann only make silk clothes for men. However, if they also make - say cufflinks - a "Men's Clothing and Accessories" keyword is more brand specific in this instance.

For example:
Brett and Mann | Men's Clothing and Accessories

SKU (Stock Keeping Unit) and Manufacturer Part Number (MPN)

A SKU is the store or product identification code. The MPN is the product's unique identification code which is part of the product's barcode. If you have them, add them to your product information. You will need them if you want to create a Google Product Feed, which we will talk about later. SKU and MPNs are also useful for generating analytic reports about product performance.

———

Adding Product Information

Product Title

This is the name you give to your product page. Your title should be maximized for SEO. You can have more than one title on your page by separating it with a dash or vertical line.

For example:

Blue Silk Shirt | Designer Shirts for Men
or
Blue Silk Shirt – Designer Shirts for Men

Here, you have created two keyword search terms, doubling the chances of your product being found by a potential consumer, if you have included these keywords or variations of these keywords in your product page.

Product Name

This will be the manufacturer product name, e.g. Silk Print Dress in Green.

URL Search Engine Friendly Names

For search engines to crawl your website effectively, you will need to use text. You do not need to have stop words in your URL (stop words are the simple words used to connect a sentence such as "and", "in", "is", and "the").

Your CMS will automatically generate a search engine friendly name when you add the product title and will even omit the stop words for you. Remember to include your keyword(s) and to avoid long search engine friendly names.

An example of a good search engine friendly product name is:

brett-mann-silk-sweater-large

This is because it is human-readable.

An example of a bad search engine friendly name would be:
btt-n-ma-142256-sk-12452

Do not use shorthand or cryptic code that only you understand. Do not include SKUs, barcode numbers and currency symbols.

Short Description
Not all shopping carts have this section. If you have it, write a caption to draw your website visitors' attention e.g. "Limited Offer. Buy one get one free!"

Full Description
Write a unique description and make it sound as natural as possible. You can repeat keyword phrases three or four times – max – in your product information page*, inclusive of your

meta title, short description, image names, alt descriptions, headlines and captions. This means that you should not repeat the keyword phrase four times in your full description, if you have included it in the product name, meta title, and your image alt description. This is known as "keyword stuffing" which will devalue your website.

Here is a description for a product called "Portable Pet Pen", with an average character count of 600:

Portable Pet Pen is ideal for small dogs and cats.
This **outdoor animal pen** will protect them from the outside environment. It has a zipper at the front for easy access. It can be neatly compacted into a bag for travel and storage. Store it away in your cupboard. Pack it in your car.

The **portable animal pen** has an open top design so that you can interact with your pet at regular intervals. It contains storage pouches for your pet's things. It comes fitted with a strong steel frame and pop up mechanism, which makes it easy to put up or down.

The **Portable Pet Pen** also has a removable fleece-pad and an easy to clean waterproof liner.

Notice that I have only used the keyword phrase

"Portable Pet Pen" twice in the description. However, I have also used the keyword variants, "Portable Animal Pen" and "Outdoor Animal Pen".

Meta Description

The meta description should be the first 255-300 characters of your **Full Description**. Note that the keyword you want to rank for should be in the first paragraph of your Full Description. Use a call to action to prompt users to click when they see it in SERPs.

Product Variants

You will use **Product Variants** to distinguish between roughly identical items which may vary in color, size, weight and dimension.

Adding Product Attributes

Attributes are characteristics specific to your product. Set up attributes to save time repeating the same information throughout your site. Your **product attributes** may include size, color, ingredients, file size (for downloadable products), etc.

Your specification attributes will show on your product page.

For example, you may have a size attribute for sweaters named "Small". You may have more than one size specification for "Small" because sizes vary between different manufacturers.

For example, below is a list of size attributes for small t-shirts made by two different manufacturers:

Chest: 49 cm (19.3 inches) Neck: 30.7 cm (12.1 inches)
Chest: 50 cm (13.3 inches) Neck: 31.7 cm (13.1 inches)

Do not forget to list your size attributes in both cm and inches.

A **checkout attribute** may be gift wrapping or a choice of delivery service, e.g. standard or next day delivery.

Number of items to display on a product page

There is nothing wrong with allowing your customers to choose the number of products displayed. The temptation, however, is to restrict the number of products shown, if you do not have many products in a category. I would not recommend doing this. Potential customers do not want to trawl through product page after product page on your website, if they can help it. They will get fed up and leave if you have twenty pages of products in one category but only display four of them at a time. Make things easy for your customers by displaying the maximum number of products per page that your CMS allows, which may be anything from 12 to 16 products at a time.

Order Displays

I would utilize the order displays to list your categories and attributes in alphabetical, or some other logical order. Correct order displays make it easier for your visitors to find their way around your website.

If you have added all your attributes in numerical order to a product, and have missed one out, or simply want to add an additional one, use negative numbers to reorder the display.

For example, I forgot to add the attribute for "Small" to this item. To make it appear at the top of my page, I have used a negative number: -1. Also, note that I have listed the sizes in a logical order, starting with the smallest first.

Attribute	**Size**	**Order Display**
Extra Small	0-2	0
Small	4-6	-1
Medium	8-10	1
Large	12-14	2
Extra Large	16	3

Weight and Measurements

There are two groups of unit systems: Metric (inches, pounds and ounces) and Imperial (centimeters and kilograms). Your CMS will have a default setting for the weight and dimensions to display to your customers. In the US, the imperial system is favored; in Europe, it is the metric system. If in doubt, stick with the default settings.

Product Checklist

- Map your categories to the product.
- Add product images.
- Write a quality meta description with a minimum of 255 characters.
- Add keywords.
- Add your manufacturer information.
- Complete your product variants.
- Display the stock quantity of the product to prevent customers purchasing items which have sold out.
- Add additional shipping costs for heavier items.
- Upload electronic files for downloadable products.
- Add related products.

Using Hreflang for Multiple Language Sites

Applying a Google hreflang to your site lets

search engines know which language or regional variations to display to your website user depending on their country. However, it will not improve your search engine ranking.

If you have a multi-language website, you will to need apply hreflang for the country you are targeting. For example, there are language variations in English speaking countries e.g. US, Canada, Great Britain, and Australia. If you want to target English speakers in Great Britain, you add the HTML code to the Header section in your code files:

<link rel="alternate" href="http://lovingclothes.com/en-gb" hreflang="en-gb" />

Here is another example for if you are in the US and want to target German speakers:

<link rel="alternate" href="http://lovingclothes.com/en-gb" hreflang="de-US" />

If your page or pages have only one English version, then you use the hreflang in this example:

<link rel="alternate" href="http://lovingclothes.com/en-gb" hreflang="en" />

Using Country Language Codes for Multiple Language Sites
The BING search engine does not use hreflang.

You will need to use country language codes in this case. Here is an example for the US:

```
<head>
<meta http-equiv="content-language"
content="en-us" />
</head>
```

It is okay to have both country language codes and hreflangs in the head section of your website.

———

Canonical URLs

Canonical URLs enhance search engine optimization for duplicate content indexed under two URLs or more. For ease of use when setting up currencies and delivery charges for your shopping cart, you may opt to have two websites one for international shipping and one for shipping within your own country, e.g. a lovingclothes.com and lovingclothes.co.uk. The content will be the same for both.

Search engines get confused when seeing the same content on multiple websites and will not know which version to rank, index, or how to direct your site link information. Your website will lose traffic and your search engine ranking will ultimately suffer.

Enable one website to be your canonical site. This will be the main website you want search engines - like Google - to rank.

Canonical URLs for Single Pages
If you want to enable canonical links for single pages, you will need to manually add the canonical link element to the code files in your File Manager. You will add it to the <head> section in your "Header" file.

For example, if you have a single blog post about trends in womenswear on your lovingclothes.com website and have the same blog post in the lovingclothes.co.uk, you can add the canonical link to the <head> section of the lovingclothes.co.uk website:

```
<link rel="canonical"
href="http://yourwebsitename/blog.com/trends-in-
womenswear"/>
```

Online Business Checklist

- Decide what you want to sell and to whom. You need to know your customer.
- Do your keyword research.
- Research your competition.
- Decide on your business branding.
- Draw up a business plan.
- Choose a domain name.
- Choose a hosting Provider.
- Choose a CMS/shopping cart application.
- Choose your web theme.
- Choose your logo.
- Add the website content and configurations settings.
- Set up your social media accounts.
- If you also have business premises, set up a **Google myBusiness** page. You can add news, offers and events to this page, and your customers can post reviews.
- Set up and run your social media and pay-per-click campaigns.
- Incorporate some competitors' analysis into your marketing strategy.
- Check your web data to see what is working and improve.

Web Task Tools

- **Trello** – tasks application
- **Asana** - for small web projects
- **Microsoft SharePoint** – document management and storage system
- **Monday** – a team management web application
- **JIRA** - for larger web projects

———

SEO

The search engine ranking of your website is largely based on the quality and unique content of your site, and the number of quality and relevant sites linking to your website and vice versa. It is therefore important that you create a quality website with good content if you want to rank high on Google's search engine as they hold more than 91 per cent of the search engine market share.

Google love brand names and high-authority websites. They love human-readable URLs. They adore images with alternative descriptions. They use a Google Panda to distinguish poor quality content from high-quality content. Poor-quality content depletes the user experience with repetitive keywords, poor navigation, less than 300 words and poor-quality graphics.

What is SEO?

SEO (Search Engine Optimization) is the process of deploying various strategies in order to increase visibility in search engines. Ultimately, you will need to figure out the user's intent in order to create helpful and relevant content. Most users conduct a search query to increase their knowledge about a particular topic or subject, to locate premises in their local area, to find a website, to complete a task, or to make a purchase.

There are a lot of ways your content can be displayed in Google's SERPs (Search Engine Results pages). These include:

- Paid ads
- Features snippets
- Image packs
- Search site links
- Product listing ads
- Knowledge panel
- Knowledge cards
- Local packs
- News packs
- Twitter cards
- Article blocks
- Local map, which includes a location map and three listed websites
- **People also ask**... – for related questions

What is important about these display types is that they appear at the top of the SERPs. So even if you get one your pages listed, you have the potential to get a crazy amount of traffic to your site.

The most important factors for organic Search Engine Optimization (SEO) are keywords and onsite optimization.

Organic traffic is traffic that comes to your website from visitors who have typed relevant search terms, known as keywords, into a search engine like Google, or Bing, as opposed to typing the website address directly into their browser. This is the method most people use to discover a website unless it is a global brand, such as Coca Cola.

Half of the traffic that comes to a website is through organic searches, about 10% is from paid search. This does not mean that you should ignore paid advertising altogether, but you should employ both disciplines to your business model.

There are three strategies to consider: keywords, building authority, and link-building.

Google has more than 200 ranking factors. Here are the important ones:

- User experience
- Relevant keywords
- High domain authority backlinks
- Page load speed
- Rich content
- Mobile responsiveness

Technical SEO Best Practices

- Make sure you have installed an SSL certificate.
- Monitor your page load speed as it affects the time it takes search engines to index. your site.
- Do not upload large resources to your site such as videos (upload these to YouTube) and image and document files.
- Compress large files before you upload them
- Upload an xml.sitemap to your server and Google's Search Console.
- Never set a page redirect on an existing redirect.
- Check the robots.txt to see that none of your pages are being blocked by search engines. You can also add directives to pages and folders that you do not want search engines to index, e.g. your admin files.
- Set up permanent 301 redirects for moved or deleted pages. This will mean that your visitors will not see a 404 error when they visit your page.
- Optimize your site for mobile devices.
- Conduct regular site audits with tools like Google Search Console, SEMrush, Screaming Frog, and Ahref.
- Only add your keyword once in your URL.
- You do not need to add short stop words in your URLs, e.g. in, the, and, it for, etc.

- Add structured data to your site using schema mark-up. Google recommends that you use JSON-LD. They provide a <u>mark-up helper tool</u> to make it easier to add structured data to your pages.
- Add noindex to links on pages that you do not want search engines to index but where you still require search engine spiders to follow the links.
- Set <meta name="robots" content="noindex, nofollow"> on any affiliate links you have added to your pages.
- Set temporary 302 redirects on pages that you have temporarily disabled due to maintenance.
- Tell search engines your preferred URL for the site by setting the rel=canonical tag in the head section of your homepage. Remember that your homepage has four urls:

    o domain.com/index.html.
    o <u>www.domain.com</u>
    o domain.com
    o <u>www.domain.com/index.html</u>.

If you are using Google Search Console, it will ask you to set your preferred domain.

Recover Lost Pages
There may come a day when you delete copy on

a web page and are unable to retrieve it. This may be your only hope. To check the history of your web page, visit:
web.archive.org

Voice Search

People are increasingly using voice search on their mobile devices to find information and products online. Combine long-tail and conversational keywords if you want to optimize for voice search. Use answerthepublic.com to discover what people are searching for on Google and Bing.

You should also add structured data to your website. A study has found that over 40% of voice search results were found using featured snippets, i.e. structured data, which you will learn more about later.

Once you know what your customers are looking for, you can create content that centers around commonly asked questions. For example, you can add a "frequently asked questions" section to the footer of your website.

Keywords

Today, more than 90% of search traffic comes from Google. They periodically change their algorithm to increase the quality of web content and increase internet security. Yes, it means that you must work harder to increase your Google rank – unless you have a truck load of money to invest in ad campaigns. Keyword stuffing, bulk directory submissions, rapid link building, are things of the past, not to mention copy and paste techniques, and buying private label rights articles. None of these will help you.

Types of Keywords
- The **Base** is the root of a keyword. For example: affiliate.
- **Modifiers** clarify the meaning of the base keyword. For example: affiliate program.
- Keyword **Extenders** further develop the meaning of the modifier with adjectives and verbs. For example: affiliate program directory. This is a long-tail keyword, which is a specific phrase that someone might search for online.

Do not go for top keywords. In short, do not target the same keywords as your competitors. The most sought-after high-ranking keywords are expensive. Instead, I suggest targeting medium rank, long-tail keywords that are relevant to your site. You will not get these keywords simply by starting to type in the Google search box and seeing what appears in its dropdown menu. Target keywords with the highest cost-per-click (CPC).

When visitors arrive at your website using one of your keyword search terms, they expect to find the products or services for that exact term. Do not tell them you sell "Diamante Collars for Cats" when you only sell "Diamante Collars for Dogs". You may get the traffic, but you will not get the sales or return visitors.

On-Page Optimization Checklist

- Your keyword phrase should be the title of your page and should be in the url and in the copy.
- Human-readable url
- A minimum of two internal links. The **anchor text** (clickable words) must not include the keyword you want to rank for
- Your page should be 600 characters (not words) long.
- You must have a least one H1 on the page. It no longer matters if you have more. You can use H1, H2, or H3 tags for your subheadings, thus breaking your

content into sections which are easier for visitors to digest.

- Add at least one image, and add your keyword phrase to the alt image tag along with its description, e.g. girl sitting in a coffee shop, **silk pink blouses women**
- Add one external link from a high-authority website. These are often well-known global brands.
- Add a 300-character meta description with a strong call-to-action.
- Use an active rather than a passive voice in your copy as it sounds more natural, e.g. **Leonard opened the shop** as opposed to **the shop was opened by Leonard**.
- Do not buy links

Keyword Research Plan

- Do your keyword research before running any SEO campaigns, or adding titles and descriptions to your website.
- Make a note of who you are trying to reach, i.e. who is your customer? Where are they in the buyers' cycle?
- Establish your keyword objectives. These should be your goals, e.g. to increase sales or to build your brand.
- Know who your competitors are and see what keywords they are using, their paid ads, and their web copy.

- Compile a list of starter keywords on an Excel spreadsheet or Google sheets. Place these into categories.
- Use ubersuggest.com to look for long-tail keywords.
- Use mergewords.com to get a combination of your base, modifiers, and keyword extenders.
- Use lsigraph.com for Latent Semantic Indexing (LSI) keywords. LSI is an algorithm that looks for relationships in the text of your content.
- Use the Google Ads Keyword Tool.
- An excellent paid keyword research tool is Moz.
- You can also invest in a web marketing suite audit tool like SEMrush.

———

Domain Authority Backlinks

External links, also known as backlinks, are imperative for ranking in the search engine result pages (SERPs). These are websites that have added one or more of your links to their website.

Domain Authority

Your domain authority is influenced by the quality of your external links. You can check your domain authority on moz.com. The Moz tool will score your website out of 100. The higher the score, the higher your website will place in search engine result pages (SERPs).

Remember that your backlinks must be trustworthy and come from high-quality reputable sites.

High-quality websites are often published on a brand domain, have positive credentials and include content written by industry experts. They will also be secure, have a unique perspective, contain no duplicate content and possess solid social cues.

Do not waste your time submitting your website to hundreds of random search engines in one go, many of which have been blacklisted because the search engines class them as spam generators. This practice will only hurt your search engine rankings. I suggest you set aside some money in your budget each month for an SEO service provider to do your directory submissions and organic backlink-building over a period. Do some research to find the best ones.

If you prefer to build your own backlinks, I advise you visit majestic.com to find reputable and trusted sites to link to your business.

Important note: removing any backlinks to your website can lead to a decrease in your web traffic. If you have "spammy" backlinks, you can contact the websites directly and ask them to remove the link.

Tips for Building Backlinks

- Create and publish quality content
- Link your blog posts and articles to your social media pages.
- Write product and service reviews for other sites.
- Write keyword-rich guest posts and comments on social networking sites, blogs, and forums.
- Try to get interviewed by other blogs and industry experts.
- Use a co-citation. This is when your

brand name appears in Google's search results. Google interprets this as a backlink.

You may want to add a useful links page to exchange links (also known as a reciprocal link) with other online businesses. Do this manually. Do not use a link trade merchant.

Important note: reciprocal linking will devalue your site if the websites you link to:

- Are not relevant to your own
- Contain poor content
- Have no page rank
- Offer products or services like yours
- Are considered as spamming websites by search engines

You can link to other high-quality websites that provide services and products that you do not offer, but are related to your business. For example, if you sell pet products on your website, you may consider exchanging links with an online retailer that provides a dog-sitting service.

- You can submit your website to the main search engines such as Google, Bing, Ask, and Yahoo. Although search engines should crawl and index your site automatically as long as your site is not blocked. Simply, search for the Submit

URL Link for each search engine and typing in your website address.
- Infographics are growing in popularity. Submit them to directories such as pitchengine.com, and marketwired.com.
- Wikipedia provides a "list of the most-popular websites". Check it out. You may find some websites among them in which you can obtain a free link e.g. Reddit, Yahoo, Wikipedia, etc.

How to Remove Bad Backlinks

Some SEO service providers will supply you with a "toxic" link report. Some web owners panic and pay the SEO service provider to upload a disavow file to Google of every link listed in the report without looking at the websites or understanding why they have been interpreted as "toxic".

Use web tools, such as Majestic, SEMrush or Ahrefs, to determine whether or not backlinks are harming your search engine rankings and/or your business. Rarely will this be the case.

However, certain backlinks can be harmful to your business. For example, if you have a vegan e-commerce business and you discover that links to your website appear on a butcher's website. This can damage your brand and reputation.

You can **email websites** and politely ask them to remove the links you do not want to appear on their site.

If you have had no response from your email requests, you can upload a **Google Disavow file**, asking Google to remove the bad backlinks.

Uploading a disavow file to Google is easy, but should only be used as a last resort. You will find the disavow file link in the Google Console.

Note: this does not guarantee the links will be removed. You may also see a drop in web traffic following a disavow.

———

Page Load Speed

If your website takes too long to load you will lose visitors. Use **Google Page Insights** to check your page load speed for both mobile and desktop. They will offer advice about improvements you can make. Aim for a page load speed of 7 seconds or less.

Tips for improving page load speed:
- If you have a cPanel, enable the "PageSpeed Optimizer"
- Set GZIP compression in your CMS if it is available, if not, install a GZIP compression plugin. This will compress large files and images.
- For WordPress, use the W3 Total Cache, Google Site Kit, and Autoptimize plugins to improve website performance.
- Free up disk space on your internal server by deleting old files and images, and files in your "temp" folder.
- Manually resize files and images before you upload them to your website.

Creating a Mobile-Friendly Website
Google rolled out Mobile-First in 2018. This means that the Googlebots will crawl your site as a mobile user first as opposed to a desktop user. This is because more people access their

website from mobile devices as opposed to desktops. If the mobile version of your website is missing links that appear on the desktop version and/or is slow to load you may see a drop in your Google ranking. If you do not have a mobile theme, or if you do not have a mobile-optimized website, the Googlebots will still index the desktop version of your site. Most CMSs will have a mobile responsive theme available. CMSs such as WordPress offer mobile plugins.

If your mobile site offers a poor user experience, use a responsive theme. A responsive theme adjusts to fit the size of the user's screen.

- Your mobile site should be easy to navigate and quick to load.
- Keep text to a minimum and do not use large images.
- Significant information should be at the top of the page.
- Call-to-action links should be prominently displayed.
- The font size should be easy to read, e.g. not too small.
- The link buttons should be easily clickable and well-spaced to avoid users clicking on the wrong links by accident. Once again, they should not be too small. Users want to browse, click and buy. They do not want to see reams of text.

The homepage should display a contact number and terms and conditions, including the shipping and returns information. The checkout process should be quick. Most people who shop from their phone do so because they are on the go, or predominantly preoccupied with something else. In short, they want to save time. They do not want to have to re-enter information or click tirelessly through page after page to complete their payment.

———

User Experience

UX Design is about designing for the user – not for yourself. Think about how a website makes you feel when you visit it for the first time. To create a strong user experience, maintain content and image consistency, web responsiveness and quick and easy navigation through continuous testing and behavioral analysis.

A modern website will increase the user experience. This should result in a lower bounce rate and an increase in conversions because it will prompt visitors to view other pages on your site.

You must first understand your buyer and why they purchase from your site. It could be that they want to make themselves feel better or they want to give back. Your ultimate aim, therefore, when designing for your user is: have I solved your problem?

Your content should be organized in a way that makes sense to the user. They should not be overwhelmed with too many choices or lose sight of the navigation through deep-links and irrelevant content.

UX Design Best Practices

- Conduct research to better understand your user.
- Use a responsive design to accommodate ease of use across mobile and desktop devices.
- Ensure that your design is consistent. Stick to 2-3 fonts and a simple colour palate of no more than 5 colors.
- Help users quickly find what they are looking for with clean and simple navigation and make sure it is more than 3 clicks away.
- Design short pages. Not ones that require you to endlessly scroll.
- Keep the main navigation visible and do not weigh it down with lots of sub-menus.
- Look at other e-commerce sites and design yours with the same elements in mind.
- Always have a generic search box. Visitors should be able to search your site without restriction.
- Add related products to your product pages.
- Do not use more than three levels of headings.
- Add fresh content to your homepage on a regular basis. This is your shop window – dress it for every occasion.

- Your content should be shareable. Add social share buttons. PDFs should be downloadable.
- Each of your pages should have a primary goal. For your product pages, this will be to make a purchase. If you have a blog, your primary goal could be to subscribe to the blog or to sign up for a newsletter.
- Do not litter your pages with lots of call-to-action links and buttons. Select the most important one and make this the main focus of your site. Two is enough for non-product pages.
- Avoid acronyms and jargon.
- Never make the word "here" a clickable link. It does not meet accessibility guidelines, is bad for SEO and offers a poor user experience. Most people know that when they hover over a link, they will see the cursor change into a hand. This tells them the link is clickable. Use a button, if it is not clear, but you do not need to signpost every link with "click here".
- Title and descriptions should be relevant to the landing page and as natural sounding as possible.
- Shorten content with bulleted lists.
- You should have the greatest amount of inbound links on your highest-ranking pages.
- Beware of cultural insensitivity when

designing for international audiences. Do not add visuals to your website that may be offensive or confusing to other cultures and countries.

- Have users test your site through a user testing company. Users can test your site remotely or through a focus group.

———

Images

Adding product images

Upload quality images. For clothing, consider using images that show the front and back of the garment and close-ups of any unique detailing on the garment. You will want to use images with a white background. This will be an image with a transparent background, i.e. a .png file extension. Most consumers will want to zoom into your image for closer inspection. Ensure that your images are not too small, or the image will become blurred as they zoom in.

Bear in mind that images that are too large may slow down the time it takes your web page to load, which can have a negative effect on your web traffic. To maximize loading time, your images should not be larger than 1 MB.

Image descriptions and names

Think carefully about the image names if you want search engines to index them correctly. Do not name images as numbers, dates or other characters which do not make sense. For search engine optimization, you may want to use other keywords rather than the product name.

Your image description could be more generic: Blue Silk Jumper Large. It does not have to necessarily, match your product description.

For example, you have an image for the product: "Brett and Mann Silky Jumper in Blue in Large". It is unlikely that your potential customers will use this search term, if they do not know the product brand.

If a customer types "blue silk jumper large" into the search engine, your product will show in the main search results as well as the image search results for "Brett and Mann Silky Jumper in Blue."

Also, complete the alt description tag (alternative description) on your shopping cart dashboard, if you are presented with it. The "alt description" is what your website visitor will read if they hover their mouse cursor over the image. The alt tag description should be user-friendly so it can be read by the visually-impaired, and human-friendly and indexed by Google. It should also include your target keyword.

Example: alt="male model wearing a blue jumper, blue silk jumper large"

Keep the text for your alt tag under 125 characters.

Adjusting images
You can use Adobe Photoshop, Adobe InDesign,

Microsoft Word 2013 (or later versions) to create a transparent background, display ads, logos, and make other image adjustments.

You can also try IrfanView. This free graphic viewer is great for quickly resizing images, adding text, and changing an image color scheme.

You can also make simple image edits using the Microsoft Paint application.

Stock photos and images
You can get additional photos and images for your website campaigns by signing up for a stock photo account. ThinkStock, Shutterstock and Adobe offer a wide range of vector illustrations, photos, videos, and images that will not dent your budget.

Check the image license for your selected images. You will need to purchase a special license if you want to use stock photos and images to produce merchandise, e.g. mugs, t-shirts, etc.

You can also get high-quality **free stock photos** from pexels.com.

Hero image
A **Hero** image has replaced the popular carousel or image slider. Some websites still use

image sliders. However, they are now considered bad for SEO in terms of page load speed and user experience.

Going forward, a large hero image or hero video is the norm. Place it at the top of your page. It should be clickable and link to a relevant page on your website. The image should be eye-catching and high quality.

You can also display seasonal and special offer images by using stock photos, e.g. Cyber Monday and Black Friday, Sale signs, Christmas images, etc. You can add special announcements, for example, the last date to place an order in time for a Christmas delivery.

Tax rules
Certain physical goods may incur tax, others will not. I suggest you check your state and locality tax laws. You may want to restrict your billing and shipping to certain countries. You can also indicate if VAT only applies to specific countries.

VAT (Value Added Tax) varies from country to country. For example, in the UK it is 20%, but in Sweden, VAT is 25% for most products.

If tax applies to specific countries, states etc., you can set the individual tax rates by country, state and postal code in the appropriate field of your CMS.

VAT for the sale of downloadable products

As of 2015, if you are selling downloadable electronic goods, you will have to use the local VAT of the countries to which you are selling and not your local VAT rate.

———

Security and Authentication

SSL Certificates

An SSL certificate enables your customers to use your website over a secure connection for their login and credit/debit card transactions. They can cost as little as £14.00 per year to as much as £870.00 per year. If you are using a secure connection, you will see a padlock icon in your website's browser, and the web address will start with "https" not "http". You will need an SSL certificate to enable a secure checkout. If possible, buy your SSL certificate from your web host provider and they will install it for you. Check the enable SSL certificate indicator in your CMS to activate the certificate on your website. Your SSL certificate provider will send you a reminder when your certificate is due to expire.

It is becoming common practice to install an SSL certificate regardless of whether your website accepts online payments, not only for web security, but also for brand credibility.

Never allow your SSL certificate to expire as Google will display an "unsecure website" message to visitors, advising them not to access your site.

Buying an SSL certificate from a third-party vendor

If you buy an SSL certificate that is not generated on your hosting provider's server, you will have to ask your hosting provider to generate a "Certificate Signing Request" on their server. They will email it to you, and then you can email it to the company from which you purchased the SSL certificate. They will then generate the correct SSL certificate for you and you can send it on to your hosting provider to install. Once they confirm the installation, you can check the "enable SSL certificate indicator" in your CMS.

Popular SSL providers include comodo.com, .123-reg.co.uk, and globalsign.com.

Note: some SSL certificates are distrusted by Google chrome. They include GetTrust, RapidSSL, and Symantec.

Do I need an SSL certificate if I am only accepting PayPal payments?

There was a time when you did not. However, PayPal have changed their stance on this, and CMS solutions are enforcing it. PayPal requires an Instant Payment Notification (IPN) that tells you about your customers transactions. In order to set this up in your CMS admin panel, you will need an https URL, i.e. one with an SSL certificate. Your customers' need to know that they are buying products over a secure website. If you are an e-commerce merchant, you should obtain an SSL certificate, regardless of what payment method(s) you offer.

Will an SSL Certificate affect my Google rank?

Yes, in a positive way. Google indexes SSL certificates. An SSL certificate installed on your website, will give your site a slight ranking boost.

Alternative Authentication Methods

You can make it easier for consumers to register and sign in to your website by offering alternative means of authentication. This means that your customers will not need to remember their passwords, and new visitors will not have to create a new user name and password, if you permit them to use their social media account information to access your site.

Offer no more than two alternative sign in/registration methods. One of these should be Facebook. (Your shopping cart software should come with a Facebook Connect plugin/extension). You should also use Google's two-factor authentication. Twitter is optional.

Captcha

Enable the Captcha program so that when visitors access certain pages of your website, they will be asked to enter a set of numbers, a combination of letters and numbers, or to identify an object in a number of photographs. This is so the program can tell if they are a human or a computer.

If you do not enable this program by entering the public and private key given to you by the Captcha provider, you will get bot spam. These bots are capable of injecting adverts in sections of your website, e.g. on the comments section of your blog page. The bots can also create multiple fake accounts on your website and use them to generate more spam.

You should have Captcha enabled on signing in and registration pages and any other pages where website visitors can leave comments and messages, such as blogs, forums and your 'contact us' form pages.

I would recommend Google's, recently updated, reCaptcha. You should be able to install and enable a reCaptcha plugin on any current CMS.

––––––

Shipping Methods

E-Commerce Shipping Best Practices
* You need to provide accurate information about your shipping times and shipping costs.
* Long shipping times increase the likelihood of shopping cart abandonment.
* Where possible offer a minimum of two methods of delivery.
* Most online shoppers know the cost of shipping an item. Therefore, do not set the cost of shipping higher than the regulated postal service prices.
* If you do not offer free shipping by default, it is a good idea to offer free shipping, or a discount, for multiple purchases.

Shipping Method Options
Your CMS will have a variety of shipping methods for you to choose from. This may include shipment by weight, UPS (United Parcel Service), USPS (US Parcel Service), and fixed rate shipping, among others.

If you want to use the shipment by weight method, you will need to research weight and cost deliveries for the countries in which you want to ship.

If you want to ship internationally and have a US-based business, you can select a fixed rate shipping method for international shipping and the USPS option for US deliveries.

If you have a UK-based business you may opt for fixed shipping costs, if you only plan to ship within the UK using the Royal Mail postal service.

Fixed Rate Shipping Costs
Although, it is not the most cost effective, this is the easiest shipping method to set.

Fixed rate shipping costs mean that your customer is charged a set amount for shipping, regardless of the price of the item or the number of items purchased.

If you opt for fixed rate shipping, but sell heavier products that will cost more to deliver, you should be able to add the additional shipping cost on the product page.

Shipping Method Information
Your shipping method information should let the customer know your method of delivery, i.e. delivery within your own country and/or overseas shipping information, and the expected date of delivery.

Here is an example of a shipping method for

United Kingdom deliveries:

Name
UK Delivery

Description
Your parcel should be delivered within 3-5 working days by Royal Mail.

Website Legal Pages

Shipping and returns

I would strongly advise you not to open your online shop without first displaying your shipping and returns information on your site. It needs to be clear and concise. You should also keep it up to date because customers can use this information as their warranty.

Shipping

- State your shipping times and methods.
- Provide the estimated dates for delivery and the shipping location.
- Provide information about your shipping costs, postage and packaging costs for both EU countries and Non-EU countries.
- If you are using a courier service, let the customer know what action the courier will take if they are not home at the time of delivery.
- State the VAT that applies for EU countries, if applicable.
- If additional costs apply for heavier items, include this information.
- If international shipping is available under another domain name you own, provide the website link.

Returns

You want to inform the customer that you will refund or exchange their item if they are not satisfied. Other relevant returns information:

- List any items that are not refundable. This might be downloadable products, or for health and hygiene, earrings and underwear. The return policy is 14 days in EU countries for physical products. If you are selling internationally, provide a 14-day policy, minimum. Ideally, you should grant the customer 30 days*.
- State that the product should be returned in the condition in which it was sent.
- You may want to ask the customer to email you to let you know they are returning an item.
- The returns address should stand out. If you are using a postal collection service for your returns, make it clear to the customer that they must state your company name on the returns package as well as the address.

*The legal return policy for digital products sold in the UK is 30 days.

Conditions of Use

This is a mandatory requirement. You will need to have this information displayed on your website if you want to open a PayPal Pro account to accept credit and debit card payments. Your Conditions of Use can be drawn up by a lawyer for a reasonable price, or you can obtain a free legal document template. Try SEQ Legal or Rocket Lawyer.

Note: you can add your Conditions of Use under the heading, Terms of Service.

The Conditions of Use may include the following disclosures:

- website access
- use of website
- website uptime
- visitor provided material
- disclaimers and limitation of liability
- user content
- links to and from other websites
- your website name and business address
- membership terms and conditions

Privacy Information

A mandatory requirement, privacy information should include:

- the disclosure of information
- the cookie law policy*
- collection of information
- data security

- potential changes to the privacy policy

*You will need to adhere to the new EU Privacy law if you are selling internationally.

GDPR

Introduced by the European Union (EU) in May 2018, General Data and Privacy Regulation (GDPR) gives customers more control over how their data is stored and used.

If you have employees in the EU and email subscribers in the EU, you will have to comply with GDPR, or face a hefty fine.

You should make it clear, in your website's privacy policy page, about how you are going to use your customers data.

You cannot share your customers email addresses with your partners or sponsors without their consent.

You cannot have a checkbox, button, or any other web control on your site that automatically opts a customer into any agreement. For example, the checkbox should be left blank and not prepopulated with a tick.

With regards to email newsletter sign-up, you can no longer automatically sign-up a customer to your newsletter because they have made a purchase or registered for an account.

The opt-in and opt-out messages should be clear, and an opt-in to a newsletter should not include a consent to share customers information.

Fortunately, the majority of CMSs and email marketing platforms have updated have created data capture options and templates in-line with GDPR.

There are also GDPR-compliant privacy policy templates available on the web. Alternatively, you can contact an attorney, or a solicitor to draw up policy documents that are unique to your business.

About Us Page
If there is a history behind your business, now is your chance to tell it. Your "about us" page gives you the opportunity to really sell your business. Make it compelling. What makes you stand out from your competitors?

Your About Us page can include the following details:

- Names of the company founders, including background and skills.

- The year in which the company was founded.
- Photographs of the company founders and other employees.
- Your Unique Selling Proposition (USP), i.e. what your business has to offer that your competitors do not.
- Qualifications and achievements related to the business.
- How the idea for your business came about.
- The process involved in making your products (if relevant).
- Check out Moz, MailChimp and Apptopia. They have some of the best About Us pages on the web.
- Your contact information
- You should display – at the very least – your customer service email address. Add a sales email address for business related enquiries.

For example:
customerservices@lovingshoppy.com
sales@lovingshoppy.com

You can also add your business telephone number and the hours and days of the week that your phone line is open for business.

If you have a physical shop or exclusive business premises, you can add your business address. You will also want to display your hours of business and a Google map showing your business location under the heading "Where to Find Us" or "How to Get There".

EU Cookie Consent Message

Cookies track users. Some of your website visitors may not want your website to track them.

If you are selling or providing a service for EU countries, you will need to display the cookie law notice. * It will show on the main page of your site and will read something like this:

"We use cookies to improve your experience on our website. By browsing this website, you agree to our use of cookies."

A check box or button is provided allowing the customer to confirm and proceed to your site. It can also include a "further info" button for more details about your cookie policy. Ensure that you display the cookie consent at the top or bottom of your website, not in the center, as this could discourage visitors from browsing.

Adding your own EU cookie notice will require you to add JavaScript files to your file Manager. You can obtain this code from websites like cookiecuttr.com and a whole host of others. However, most shopping cart software comes with EU cookie consent files as standard.

Emails

Set up your email accounts on your own domain name through the free webmail accounts provided by your hosting provider. They will appear on your virtual web hosting account dashboard, e.g. cPanel. Alternatively, you can use other webmail services. While they may offer more features, you will normally have to pay a separate monthly charge for them.

You should have more than one business email address. You can have one for admin, one for sales, one for customer services, one for yourself, and one for each of your employees.

Tip: For manageability, set up a Gmail account in your business name and then forward all your business emails to the Gmail account. You can arrange them in separate folders if you wish.

Once you have set up your email addresses, you can add them to the email accounts settings on your CMS.

- Add your email address, e.g. customerservices@yourwebsitename.com
- Your host webmail provider, e.g. mail.yourwebsitename.com
- Your port number will normally be 25. If

you are unsure of the port number, check with your hosting provider
- Your email name, e.g. Customer Services
- Your email username can be the same as your email address,
- e.g. customerservices@yourwebsitename.com

Email Custom Signatures

Set up custom signatures and messages for your email addresses to save time when drafting replies. You can have multiple ones for a variety of scenarios.

For example:

Dear Customer,

We are writing to let you know that your order is on its way and can no longer be changed. If you would like to manage or return an item, please refer to the invoice enclosed with your order.

Your estimated delivery date is:

Monday 20th Mar 2020 – Wednesday 23rd Mar 2020

Yours sincerely,

John Smith
yourwebsitename.com
0845-000-000-111

Your email subject headers should also be clear, e.g. "Your item has been dispatched", "About your order", "Thank you for your enquiry", etc.

Note: not all free webmail providers give you the option of setting up multiple custom signatures. I suggest you ask your hosting provider which of their webmail providers offer this feature.

———

Payment Methods

If you are selling physical products, I would recommend you give customers the option of paying by PayPal and by credit/debit card as consumers do not want to get to the checkout only to find that you do not facilitate their payment method.

Display payment method graphics in the footer of your website and/or in the top right-hand corner of your website. If you are only selling digital products and/or services, a PayPal Standard checkout will suffice.

PayPal Direct Method and PayPal Pro
The easiest way to accept credit and debit cards on your website is to open a PayPal Pro account. It costs approximately £24.00 per month/$30.00. You will also have to pay merchant fees of 2.9% plus US $0.30 per transaction.

This is what is also known as a PayPal Direct method. Customers who pay with this method will be unaware that PayPal facilitates their payments and they will not be required to sign into PayPal or open a PayPal account during the checkout process.

If you set up a PayPal Pro account, you need to have your website set up. To open a PayPal Pro account your privacy notice, shipping and returns information and conditions of use must be displayed on your website. PayPal will check this before they approve your account.

Your shopping cart should give you the option of recuperating your merchant fees by charging them as an additional fee to the customer when they opt to pay by credit/debit card. It is rare for stores to do this. Customers do not like to purchase products only to find there is an extra charge waiting for them when they go to checkout because they're paying by credit or debit card.

To connect your website to PayPal Pro, PayPal will provide you with API credentials: a name, password and signature, which you will add to the assigned text box fields in your CMS dashboard.

PayPal Standard Method

PayPal Standard allows customers to sign into their PayPal account to make their payment. A standard PayPal account does not incur a monthly subscription fee. It also includes a mobile checkout and built-in fraud protection.

Did you know that it also allows non-PayPal customers to pay with their credit card? Consumers who do not know how PayPal works and do not have a PayPal account, may not realise this and will abandon the checkout process when they see they are being directed to PayPal.

If you are selling physical products, configure your website for both PayPal Standard and PayPal Direct methods.

If you are selling downloadable products only, use PayPal Standard for a quick and cost-effective checkout.

To connect your website to PayPal Standard, PayPal will provide you with a PDT Identity Token, which you can add to the assigned field in your CMS dashboard along with the business email address you used to set up your PayPal account. Do not forget to turn on Instant Payment Notification so that PayPal can notify you when someone has purchased a product from your store.

———

Customer Retention

If you want to reduce your bounce rate and retain customer loyalty, make your website sticky. This means providing enough interesting and unique content to make your visitors stick around. Consider including the following on your website:

News

As an alternative to a blog, you can have a news page. A news page is easier to write than a blog. You can publish news about your products, special offers, and events. However, blogs are the more popular choice.

Blogging

Blog posts can be time-consuming if you are running your own website. If you have room in your budget to employ someone to write blog posts for you, then I would suggest you do this.

If you want to write your own blog posts, put a content strategy in place. Think about your objectives, e.g. to sell, to increase engagement, etc.

The content should be unique and no less than 300 words. I would aim to write anywhere between 600-2000 words. You can post blogs about your products and other related topics. For example, if you sell fish tanks, you may want to post a blog about a species of fish, or a scuba diving expedition involving your company. You can include relevant links and images to a few products on your website to prompt blog visitors to buy them.

To increase exposure on the internet, publish blog articles on e-zine websites, e.g. ezinearticles.com. To get more traffic, you can add your website link to the bottom of your e-zine article. Publish your unique content article on your selected e-zine website before you publish it on your website.

Share Buttons
It is imperative you have these on your website. Share buttons or smart buttons, as they are also known, allow you to post and share your products, services, blog, and news events directly from your website.

They also allow visitors to share your web content across their social media platforms, and email their friends and family about your products and services. This is great free advertising. Not only will it raise brand awareness and increase your web traffic, it can also help build organic backlinks.

If visitors frequently share your content across the web it sends strong social signals to Google, which means they will show your content more often.

If your CMS has a smart button feature built-in, you can share your new products through your social media outlets as soon as you have added them to the page.

If your CMS does not come with share buttons, you may be able to get them in the form of a plugin. Check with your CMS provider.

Alternatively, you can obtain share buttons through the **AddThis** sharing website. This will require you to add additional JavaScript code to your site. You can ask your webmaster or web developer to add this sharing code, if you lack the experience to do so.

The top share buttons every website should have:

- Facebook
- Twitter
- Reddit
- LinkedIn
- Email (for visitors who do not have social media accounts).

Where to place Share Buttons
Display share buttons on the left side of your website, at the bottom of your blog and news posts, and/or on your product pages.

Reviews

Reviews are an indisputable way to increase conversions, gain consumer dependability, and business credibility.

There are several ways to obtain credible reviews: through Trust Pilot, your Facebook page and through a "Google My Business" page. These reviews will show in the search results for your business. Never buy or post fake reviews as these can ruin your business. Try to get into the habit of responding to reviews (good or bad) to promote trust, loyalty, and to show that you active in your business.

You can also display reviews and testimonials on your website. For e-commerce, enable the product reviews feature in your CMS.

Try to keep your reviews current and display your recent reviews first. Consumers have little interest in old reviews, no matter how good they are.

Newsletters

If you want to get more customers and retain customer loyalty, ask your customers to sign up for your newsletter. Place the "Sign Up" form on your homepage. You can send your newsletter subscribers information about new products, special offers and events.

To attract more visitors to sign up, offer them a gift, discount, reward points, etc.

You can also include customer testimonials and product reviews in your newsletter.

Do not provide important information about your products in an image because these images will not actually show up in the email. Email providers have this feature turned off by default.

Reward Points

Reward Points help build customer loyalty. A reward point can be the equivalent of a £1/$1 or less. You can offer a fixed amount of reward points for customers who purchase items from your store for the first time. You can also offer points when a customer registers on your store.

Do not forget to set your point system to remove reward points when an order is cancelled.

Virtual Gift Cards

If your customers are looking for a gift and cannot make up their minds what to purchase, a virtual gift card is ideal. As it is virtual, the customer need only pay for its value. Offer them on your website with a minimum, mid-range, and maximum value. You can create your own virtual gift card or use royalty-free images.

For example, your Product Name for your virtual gift card can be "$10 Gift Card".

However, the search-engine-friendly URL name should not include the currency symbol. In this case, the "$" symbol.

If your shopping cart has a Gift Card facility built-in, remember to indicate that your product is a **Virtual Gift Card** as opposed to **a Physical Gift Card.**

Wishlists

This handy feature allows customers to add products to a wish list, or email their wish list to friends and family. They can then purchase these items later, if they desire.

Polls

A poll plugin asks multiple choice questions to your website visitors and displays the results in percentages.

You can engage with your customers by adding a poll to your website and displaying the results. If you decide to add a poll, make it interesting and beneficial. For instance, asking a website visitor for their favorite color isn't likely to make them stay on your website for long.

Take this example: if you have an online denim store, you can ask the customer how many pairs of blue jeans they brought last year. A poll like this will give you an insight into the number of customers buying jeans, and you can adjust your stock to match this correlation. Your poll will also leave the customer asking themselves: did I buy too many or not enough? Should I purchase a pair of jeans in another color? Or your poll may simply serve as a reminder to the customer that they need to purchase a new pair of jeans, which they can do from your website.

Alternatively, you can add an exit poll to your website, to ask visitors why they are leaving your site.

You can also use polls as part of your social media strategy.

Chat
Live Chat
Live Chat windows are another way for you to engage with visitors to your site. Live Chat has the highest rate of customer satisfaction and customers are more likely to buy after a chat.

To ensure visitors have a pleasant and memorable experience that will encourage them to buy, offer solutions. If a requested product is out of stock, offer an alternative. Be professional and friendly, and check for typos.

Live Chats will also teach you more about your

customers behavior and what you can do to improve as visitors are more likely to voice their shopping experience on your website prior to converting.

Chatbots

Chatbots use AI (Artificial Intelligence) technology to automate frequently asked questions and customer interactions. Because they do not rely on a response from a human, customer service response times are increased. Ideal for small and medium-sized businesses, chatbots help cut down on customer email enquiries and costs, helps customers discover your products and services, helps you identify your costumers needs, and assist in driving sales, by selling to the customer, during the chat process.

You can get Chatbot plugins for websites. You can also use Chatbots on Facebook and Twitter as part of your marketing strategy.

Get a feel for Chatbots by checking out Facebook Messenger and other e-commerce websites that utilize Chatbots.

Videos

You should create a YouTube channel to showcase brand promotional videos, and to display products and events on your website.

Web Content

These days, content and engagement is king. And not just any content. I am talking about unique, well written, rich content. It should sound natural. If you get your products from a dropshipper, or an established online retailer with a wholesale account, do not copy and paste their descriptions into your own website to save time; all this will do is downgrade your site.

Google will penalize you if you have thin content on your web pages. You can check for penalties in the manual action section of Google Search Console tools. Thin content is duplicate content that is found on the site or auto-generated content. You should also avoid "doorway pages", purposely written with keyword terms for search engines, but they don't make much sense to the reader.

Use structured data such as rich snippets and rich cards to control how you want your web pages to appear in Google's search results. We will discuss more about these later.

Types of content

- Infographics
- Videos
- Apps
- PDFs
- Microsites
- Images
- Quizzes
- Articles
- Surveys
- Polls
- Blogs
- Podcasts
- eBooks

Where to Find Content

- Use **Buzzsumo** and **Google Trends** to find trending topics.
- Set up Google Alerts on topics relevant to your business. You can sift through them when they arrive in your Gmail inbox and then add them to your tweeting schedule.
- Take content from other social media platforms and personalize it with a comment of your own.

How to Set up Google Alerts

To set up Google Alerts, login into google.com/alerts. Search for the keyword terms for which you want to receive alerts, and how frequently you would like to receive them. Any news about your chosen topics will be sent to your Gmail account. You can use the information to keep up-to-date with your chosen niche, share it your social media platforms, build backlinks, and network with other people/businesses with the same interests.

Connect with Influencers

Find out who is sharing your content. Do some outreach work to connect with influencers: these can be celebrities', or people who are passion about your products and/or website. Ask them for an interview. You can then mention them in one of your articles. Their mention can help increase sales.

Connect with influential bloggers, relevant to your niche and ask them to write a blog post about your products or business. You can offer them a free product or discount in return.

—

Marketing

Promoting your business online requires strategies for your customer, your business, and your marketing channels.

Your business strategies should encompass your mission statement, your goals, what makes you stand out from your competition, and an elevator pitch that explains your brand concept. You need to know where your customers are online, how you can find them and how they can find you.

Audience considerations:

- Age range
- Gender
- Interests
- What online platforms do they use? e.g. Yahoo, Bing, Snapchat.
- Needs, i.e. what problem are they trying to solve?

You will probably find you have different audiences. You will need to divide these audiences into segments. Consider your goals for each of these segments, and if you can meet their needs.

You do not need to use all marketing channels to promote your business. Most of your traffic will come from organic search. It is how your customers find you online, especially if you are still building your brand. The quickest way to drive traffic to your business is through paid advertising. However, if you work on building your social media channels and SEO on your website, you can increase conversions and reduce your paid advertising spend.

Give your customer a positive experience. Think about how they will navigate through your site and the messages you will need to supply to move them along the sales funnel.

On-site Marketing

- Search Engine Optimization (SEO)
- Press releases
- Social Media marketing,
- Content marketing, e.g. articles, blogging, etc.
- Paid advertising
- Influencer marketing
- Google shopping channel
- Email marketing
- Business partnerships and sponsors
- Affiliate marketing

- Webinars
- Podcasts
- Videos

Off-site Marketing

- Trade fairs and conferences
- Events
- Workshops and conferences
- Business partnerships and sponsors
- Posting ads in physical magazines and newspapers
- Telemarketing

———

Content Marketing

Google prefers long-word content (minimum of 2,000 words). If you have an e-commerce site, this will not apply to your product pages but you can certainly create long-word content for your press releases, blogs, articles, product category, and brand pages. You can gain a lot of free backlinks with high-quality content.

Good content marketing involves engagement, distribution and a call-to-action. It must be valuable and show authority.

Defining a Content Marketing Strategy

1. Define your purpose and set a S.M.A.R.T goal.

What do you want to achieve from your content marketing campaign? Consider the following:

- Do you want to increase sales?
- Do you want to build brand awareness?
- Is your main goal to build leads?
- Do you need to collect information?

2. Define your audience persona.

Your content needs to be personalized for your audience. Collecting data helps. Build an avatar of your target visitor.

3. Identify the types of content you want to create.
4. Publish and distribute your content. You can do this through the following mediums and channels:

- Newsletters
- Pinterest
- Facebook
- Forums
- Press releases
- eBook publishing platforms
- YouTube videos
- Quora
- Influencer outlets
- PDFs
- SlideShare
- StumbleUpon
- Twitter
- Snapchat
- Reddit
- Instagram
- Article sites

Content Marketing Tips

- Write persuasive content.
- Tell a story and make it relatable.
- Copy should be conversational and not too wordy.
- Write as if you are addressing one

person, i.e. your customer.

- Search for what is trending.
- Gain insights with surveys and polls
- Create content with the keywords that drive content to your site. You can get these keywords from your **Google Search Console** account.
- Create your seasonal content months in advance, not a couple of weeks before launch. This will give it time to build momentum in search engines.
- Use psychological power words, e.g. free, you easy, simple, proven, instant, today, etc. These words are shown to catch a reader's attention.
- Write as if you are an expert. Establishing authority and building trust, will help you generate leads and sales, and give you a higher return on investment than traditional advertising.
- Write a strong headline. Note, that for blogs and articles, headlines with numbers, tend to perform better than those with all letters.
- Your intro copy should be relevant to your headline.
- Content should be broken into chunks to make it easier to consume.
- Your call-to-actions should be clear and prominent.
- Create content for each buyer stage. It could be relevant to your demographic,

e.g. age, location, etc. Map out these stages in terms of interactions. You can see how your customer interacts with your content through your social media statistics and Google's tracking tools.

- Repurpose content into other formats, e.g. PDFS, eBooks, slides, infographics, etc.

Press Loft

If you have an e-commerce site, upload your product photos to pressloft.com. Press Loft is an all-in-one online press room. Journalists and influencers will download the ones they like and promote them across the web. Sign up for a free trial and upload your product images.

If journalists and influencers download a good number of your product images while on a trial, then it is worth considering signing up for a paid account. If none are downloaded, it might be that the images are poor quality, too generic, or not visually-appealing. For example, household tools as oppose to cute dog coats.

Tools for Researching Trends

- Search Metrics
- Google Trends
- Google Keyword Search
- Google Ads

To view the number of unique visitors to your website, and obtain other useful statistics about your website visitors, set up a Google Analytics account for your domain name.

Other tools you can try are:
- sysomo.com
- sproutsocial.com

If you want to become an Influencer and find trending topics, try Quora. You can set up a user profile on their site. Answer questions and comment on topics relevant to your area of expertise.

Create a social media content calendar and repost high-performing content.

———

Social Media

I would recommend opening, minimally a Twitter and Facebook account. You may also want to set up a Pinterest, Instagram, and YouTube account. Choose which is relevant for your business. I would advise you not to have social media links just for the sake of it. Make use of your social media accounts and learn how to use them to your advantage. Depending on the nature of your business, some may work better than others.

Keep the branding consistent across all your social media platforms. Use the same logos and make sure that your posts are in keeping with the tone of your business.

Useful Social Media Tools

- buffer.com
- hootesuite.com
- buzzsumo.com

How to Build Positive Sentiment

- Use visuals, e.g. infographics, cute animals, etc.
- Run a video series or podcast
- Offer a free download
- Run a contest

- Write how-to-articles

Twitter

Twitter success requires a content strategy. Use it in conjunction with another social media platform like Facebook. Your aim should be to generate multiple interactions, gain more followers, and have your followers share your content.

You need to make your Twitter followers feel as if they are part of a community. Do not go for the hard sell and keep tweeting about your business, unless you are promoting a special offer or event. Instead, sell the lifestyle associated to your business.

Tips for Twitter Success

- Try to add unique content and not just generic content you find on the internet.
- Each tweet should include no more than 3 relevant hashtags.
- Be careful not to post anything controversial or make any negative comments.
- Retweet followers' posts
- Use a social media scheduling application like Buffer or Hootsuite to automatically post your tweets.
- Use Bitly to shorten your web links.

(This will not be necessary if you are using Buffer).
- Use your mobile to tweet on the go.
- Interact with users with many followers.
- Use Twitter advertising to get more followers, or to try to sell a product.
- If you are interested in launching paid campaigns on this platform, use Twitter's **Promoted Trends** to advertise your content.
- To maximize effectiveness, tweet a minimum of 5 times a day.
- Use Twitter analytics to measure your performance and find potential influencers.

Content to Tweet?

The type of content you want for Twitter are visuals, such as videos and images, inspirational quotes, and seasonal themes. Tweet about:

- Special deals, promotions and events.
- Ask your followers for their point of view on a topic.
- Comment on what is trending to increase engagement.
- Share an insight into your work life and that of your employees.

Facebook

There are many benefits to having a business Facebook page:

- If your CMS has a Facebook shop plugin, customers can shop directly from your Facebook page. Alternatively, you can create a shop - from scratch - on your Facebook page.
- You can list special offers and events.
- You can promote your website through paid advertising and get real traffic and customers for your website.
- You can utilize Facebook Live Authority video streaming to connect to your followers and grow your brand. With over 1 billion Facebook users, video marketing on this social media platform is a popular and smart business choice. The video streaming market will be worth 70.05 billion dollars by 2021.
- In terms of pay-per-click, Facebook offers more precise targeting due to detailed information that can be gathered from the user's profile page.

Most of your Facebook content will be made up of images and videos indirectly related to your business, and a few unrelated but interesting posts. Do not publish text-only posts. They do not convert well in terms of sales. Post 2-3 times a day only.

To increase customer engagement and to get more followers for your page, use promoted and boosted ads.

Use multi-product and offer ads to boost sales. Multi-product ads are powerful because they let visitors browse a selection of your products in one ad. Bear in mind, you can get both likes, followers and sales from running offer and multi-product ads only.

Use Facebook Insights to obtain detailed information about your target audience and to track your conversions.

Repeat what works through testing. Set up a maximum of five low cost ads with varying target audiences, visuals and ad descriptions to see which ad (or ads) result in the highest conversions.

Facebook Advertising
Facebook paid advertising lets you target and refine your demographic. They are good for retargeting visitors and can be cheaper to run.

How successful your Facebook ads are will depend on your budget, your audience demographic and the quality of your ad.

If you are just starting out, the focus of your ad should not be product-based. You need to focus on the message. Think about what makes you unique and what problem you are trying to solve. Look at your competitors Facebook pages.

You can create a brand-new ad or one based on a successful post (successful in terms of engagement likes and comments).

There are several settings needed to run a Facebook ad:

- **Schedule** – how long you want your ad to run
- **Budget** – the amount you can afford to pay for an add
- **Bid** – the maximum amount you are willing to spend for a person to click, view or supply their email address
- **Placement** – where you want your ad placed. This could be desktop or mobile.
- **Creative** – do you want your ad to be a video or an image?

For your first e-commerce Facebook ad, offer a discount and send visitors to your product or category pages with a strong call-to-action button, e.g. buy now.

Steps to Facebook Ad Success

1. Set your conversion objective: store traffic, catalog sales or store traffic.

2. Do A/B split testing to see which ad is the highest performing. Then reset your budget and image for the best performing one.

3. Add your billing information. If you set up a payment threshold, you will be billed at the end of the month or you can be billed at the end of your campaign.

4. Understand your buyer's behavior

    - Target your audience – use Facebook's Audience Insights to build a profile for your audience by learning their preferences, demographics and buying behaviour.
    - Look at your existing audience preferences and make a note of these. What devices are they are on? Where are they located?
    - When considering demographics by location, exclude areas that your competitors are targeting.
    - Use the Advanced menu to further narrow down your audience.

5. Choose your ad type:

    - **Lead ads** – run these to collect email addresses of mobile users.
    - **Instant Experience** – these are full

screen, fast loading ads.

- **Sales Collection ads** – exclusively for mobile, people can view your ads side-by-side.
- **SlideShow ads** – these allow you to run videos and images that do not use a lot of bandwidth.
- **Carousel ads** – you can add up to 10 video clips, and or photos.
- **Video ads** – use these to show off your brand. Show lifestyle and aspiration.
- **Photos ads** – for e-commerce choose six images not one to promote your ad.
- **Dynamic ads** are based on the target audience from Facebook

6. Select where you want your ad to show – on desktop or mobile. If you select mobile, you have the option of displaying your ad on Instagram.

7. Set up your schedule. Choose when the ad will end and set a daily budget. This should be a low figure. How long do you want your ad to run? You have three campaign options to choose from: CPC, CTC or CPM. Cost per impression is the cost per thousand impression amount paid, by 1000 views. Remember impressions are the number of times your ad is shown. The same person can see

your ad more than once, so these 1000 views are not unique individuals.

Instagram

Today, most digital businesses use Twitter and Facebook to increase their reach across the web. They are considered crucial social media platforms for small and large businesses alike. In recent years, Instagram has become an effective platform for driving online sales. Its demographic is 18 to 34-year-olds. It allows users to share pictures and short 60 second videos (or in the case of Instagram Stories, 15 second videos).

A new addition is Instagram TV (IGTV) which allows users to upload videos of up to 1 hour in length to their Instagram account.

Instagram now generates more followers than Twitter and now has over 800 million users. There are several reasons for this. First and foremost, Instagram is about visuals – not words. Conversion rates are higher for videos and images than text because they offer immediate gratification and appeal to people's emotions. Secondly, more users access the web via their mobile devices. With many more consumers shopping from their mobile devices, online businesses can benefit from using Instagram to sell their products, connect with their customers, find new ones and build brand awareness.

Facebook owns Instagram. This means that you can run your business ads through the Ads Manager on your Facebook page.

If you are a small business, you can set up a personal Instagram account and still run your ads on Facebook to show on both social media platforms. You can also set up Facebook Pixels to track your conversions and set up retargeting ads for individuals who visited your site but did not make a purchase.

Furthermore, you can still share your Instagram pictures across Twitter, Facebook, Flickr, and Tumbler.

Instagram Tips and Best Practices

- Work with Instagram influencers. They will sponsor you and promote your business in return for a free product or service.
- Connect your website to a shoppable storefront such as have2have.it, which will send visitors to your e-commerce site via your Instagram profile. Another is readypulse.com. Do some research as the list is growing.
- You can also create a free online shop using Inselly. Add the hashtag #inselly

to your posts. This allows Instagram to identify your content as shoppable. You could use it to push some of your discounted or discontinued stock.

- Add music to your Instagram content to make it more appealing.
- Be creative. Post a variety of images and videos. Only 20% of your posts should consist of hard-selling your business.
- Run and track your Instagram ads through Facebook's Ad Manager.
- Run Instagram contests to connect with followers and sell your product. Try out some contest tools e.g. Gleam or WooBox.
- Use iconosquare.com to monitor your analytics and help manage contests.
- Create a series of posts with Instagram Stories.
- Upload videos to IGTV that showcase your products. Here, you can add links to your website. Do not forget to include a call to action.
- Make use of inspirational or motivational captions.
- Add pictures of your followers with your products in your Instagram posts. Remember to get their permission first.
- Provide a link to your website in your bio and a keyword rich description.
- Give your followers exclusive previews of your products. You can showcase a new product using Instagram's Marquee

features.
- Like your followers' posts.
- Ask your followers to tag your friends.
- Photos should be high-resolution. You can edit photos directly from your phone. There are several mobile apps you can use with additional editing features.
- Add a touch of personal-branding. Your posts can include photos of yourself and your employees at work gatherings.
- Increase your reach through hashtags. Use popular hashtags in your video and picture descriptions.
- Unlike Twitter and Facebook, the more hashtags you use, the further your Instagram reach. Aim for 11 hashtags per post. (30 is the limit).
- Remember, you do not need to post every day.
- To make your photos more accessible, ensure that you have added Alt text.
- Ensure that you include a relevant call to action in your post, e.g. "download it here".
- You can schedule your Instagram posts through social media management platforms such as Hootsuite and Buffer.
- Do not download pictures from the internet and try to pass them off as your own.

YouTube

Set up a YouTube channel to create and publish videos of your products and events, to display affiliate marketing material, and to tell more people about your business.

Product videos can include reviews, product unveiling, or product comparisons. If you are selling digital goods, such as eBooks, you can publish book trailer videos. Try Fiverr.com, if you are looking to produce a promotional video at a relatively cheap cost. (You will need to purchase the license copy for both the visual and soundtrack).

You can also make some serious revenue through video marketing. More people than ever are watching videos online for educational, inspirational and entertainment purposes. Videos are easy to find online and easy to search for on any mobile device. If you want to tap into this market, you will need to learn the strategy that will make people click on your ads as oppose to your competitors and how to create cost effective high-quality videos.

YouTube Paid Advertising

It makes sense to advertise your business on the world's second largest search engine. Owned by Google, YouTube lets you run cost-effective ads that will drive sales, allow you to connect with your audience and build brand awareness.

Research has shown a 40% yearly growth of YouTube advertisers.

The benefits of advertising on your YouTube is that you only pay if a viewer watches the first 30 seconds of your video.

There are several types of YouTube Ads:

- Pre-roll ads are the ones that are shown at the start of a video a user has selected to play. They cannot be skipped.
- Bumper ads are 6 seconds long and optimized for mobile because they cannot be skipped
- **True View Discovery** ads that are triggered by keywords users input in the YouTube browser and will be displayed at the top of the search results
- **TrueView Instream** ads play before someone watches a video and between ads. Users can skip these ads after 6 seconds.

There are a variety of video ads you can create:

- Testimonials
- Product launches
- Website opening
- Events
- Product demos

- Business and/or product commercials

It is easy to create a YouTube channel

- Sign into YouTube with your Gmail account.
- Click on your profile in the upper-right corner
- Select "Your channel" to create your channel.
- Click on the **Customize Channel** button. From here, you can add your description, channel·art, and links.
- From the Customize Channel page, you can access the **Creator Studio** by clicking on your channel profile in the upper right-hand corner

The Channel Dashboard is where you upload and manage your videos, view your analytics and manage your settings.

- Click on Settings in the left navigation
- Select Channel
- Click on the **Advanced Settings** tab
- Select **Advanced Channel Settings**. This is where you can add your YouTube to your Google Ads account. All YouTube advertising is created in Google Ads

You can choose a video for your campaign in Google Ads, once you have uploaded it to

YouTube. For your ad to run, you will need to add a final URL, display URL, call-to-action and a headline. You also have the option of selecting your audience demographics, e.g. age, gender, etc, and where you want your ads to be placed, i.e. websites, YouTube, popular content, YouTube Channels and YouTube videos. Ideally, you will want them shown in all locations Google has to offer.

Tips for YouTube Advertising

- Create a retargeting list based on your YouTube viewers, viewing history.
- Create 2-3 different variations of your video.
- Your call-to-action should take visitors to your website.
- Start with a brand awareness campaign or product launch video.
- Track your YouTube analytics. This will help you better target your ads.
- Start with a small budget of $10-$15 dollars per day or $50 for a campaign total.
- Need help with video creation? You can use Animoto's cloud-based video creation service.
- Use Camtasia Studio for recording and editing your videos.
- To build brand awareness and to generate leads, use instream ads

- For sales, use TrueView for Shopping. You will need to link your Google Merchant feed to your video campaign. When your video ad, cards containing images of your products will be shown underneath with a link to take buyers directly to your store to make a purchase.

Tips for YouTube Success

- Keep your video titles below 50 characters.
- Add 200-350-word descriptions and a call-to-action links.
- Embed your YouTube videos in your website to increase viewability.
- Create a YouTube channel and grow your subscribers through content marketing and paid advertising.
- You can find your YouTube keywords by typing them into the YouTube browser. Word-for-word match keywords perform better on YouTube.
- Add between 30 to 40 keyword tags.
- Produce videos longer than 6 mins and less than 20 for a good ranking in YouTube, and to get more views.
- Produce engaging videos; the longer a user views your video the better you will rank.
- Use **End Cards** and **End Screens** to

increase engagement and/or promote your other videos and playlists, ask watchers to subscribe to your channel, to visit your website, to promote another channel, or to participate in a poll.

- Share your YouTube videos on your other social media channels and in your email campaigns.
- Reach out to influencers to promote your products on their channel in return for a product, discount or fee.

LinkedIn

Owned by Microsoft, LinkedIn has over 500 million users. It is used for professional development and career progression. It has a learning platform and provides resources and global organisation information.

It is not a social networking platform that people associate with retail marketing. However, it is a common platform for B2B (business-to-business) marketing. Over 90% of B2B marketers use LinkedIn, and research has shown that B2B websites receive 50% of their traffic from LinkedIn.

It is popular with US companies and generates three times more conversions than Twitter or Facebook. It is also more targeted and cheaper than Google Ads.

LinkedIn is a great place to generate leads. The LinkedIn InMail boxes receive more opens than regular email boxes. This is because LinkedIn members do not need to create a sign-up form.

What can I do on LinkedIn?

- Video marketing.
- Product launches and events.
- Subscription-based learning with video tutorials from industry experts.
- Set up **Company Pages** from your personal account.
- Post your job vacancies or headhunt potential employees for your business.
- Discover influencers and thought leaders.
- Drive business through sponsored content and in-mail ads.
- It supports retargeting and an audience network. The audience network are websites that display LinkedIn ads and can generate an 80% increase in clicks.
- Create SlideShare presentations.
- Generate leads with lead gen forms.

How to Create a LinkedIn Company Page

To create a company page, you first need to create a company account. However, you do not need to have a company to create a company page.

To create a company page, you will also need your company address/location, your name, email address, and website URL.

Navigate to the top menu in your LinkedIn profile and click on **Work**. Scroll down to **Create a Company Page.**

Create a company update and choose if you want to share your update with just your followers or the public.

When you post a company update, a **Sponsor Now** button will appear, giving you a paid advertising option. This is similar to the 'boost' post, you would see on Facebook. You can also access the Campaign Manager through "Work", which you will find in the top menu.

Like all paid platforms, you will also be able to view your metrics and set your budget.

LinkedIn Groups
Use LinkedIn groups to build your mailing lists. You can then send invites to people in your industry. Note, that they will only receive your invites if they have notifications turned on.

To build a mailing list from LinkedIn, click in the LinkedIn search bar and select **People** and then **All Filters**. Here, you will find potential leads to add to your contact list.

Tips for LinkedIn Success

- Think about the strategy you want to employ for your business. Use **Gen Forms** to get leads. To drive traffic, use text ads to direct visitors to your content and website. Publish videos to create engagement.
- You will need to publish at least 10 pieces of content before seeing a conversion.
- Publish posts directly on the LinkedIn platform. Self-contained posts perform better than posts that come from an external link.
- You can target certain countries or industries easily by uploading your own email lists or importing them through a CRM (Content relationship Manager System) like Salesforce.
- Include a call-to-action in your posts.
- Make use of engaging videos to showcase your products and services.
- Add an eye-catching banner to your company page.
- Add a **Follow** button to your ad.
- Target your audience by uploading your email list.

- Make use of LinkedIn plugins. They are usually available for most CMSs', including WordPress.
- Repurpose your content on SlideShare.
- Share statistics and infographics.
- Comment on competitors updates.
- Your audience should be included in the headline of your post, e.g. tent suppliers.
- Create **Showcase Pages** to promote various products or different aspects of your business.
- Check the website demographics in the campaign manager to ensure that you are reaching your target customer.
- Make sure your personal business profile is completed in full, and encourage your employees to complete theirs. You can also ask them to share your company's content in their posts.
- Join groups in your industry to build your network.
- Post company updates once or twice a day.

LinkedIn Tools

- Crystalknows – social personality platform
- eLinkPro – automated to visit 800 Linkedin profiles.

- <u>LeadFuze</u> – social prospecting tool to collect leads
- <u>LinkedProspect</u> – prospecting automation software for bulk messaging and invites.

Snapchat

Snapchat is popular amongst the under-30s. It has more than 190 million daily users. It is a great advertising platform and is popular with brands.

Users communicate and share information with pictures and videos.

Most brands use Snapchat to launch new products.

The marketing strategy here is to create a buzz by creating imaginative stories. Snapchat displays these stories for 24 hours.

Snapchat paid advertising campaigns are very effective, but they are not cheap. One campaign could cost you over $2500/£2000.

Snapchat Marketing Tips

- Give access to live events.
- Give users exclusive offers. Post promotion codes, contests and

giveaways. You can post these on your website and other social media pages to encourage Snapchatters to follow you.

- Use captions and emojis to make your stories stand out.
- Engage with Snapchatters and encourage them to post videos and pictures of themselves using your product. Offer them a discount or a free product in return.
- Add your Snapchat user name to your website along with your Snapchat QR code (machine-readable barcode). You can create your QR code in Snapchat. This code will help you get more followers and allow you to connect with other Snapchatters.
- Display your QR code on your other social media platforms, business cards and other promotional material.
- Use Snapchat's **Lens Studio** app to create virtual reality experiences and propel your advertising strategy.
- To get followers, find out what is trending on Snapchat and create similar content to share on Snapchat and your other social media platforms.
- Post at fixed times of the day to maximize your reach.
- To get an idea of what works, check out brand name, Snapchat successes.

Pinterest

Pinterest has about 250 million users. It is an app that displays images to give users ideas and inspiration. It is good for indirect sales and driving traffic. It also gives a good insight into product trends.

Open a Pinterest business account. Add your website link, description and profile picture to your page.

Tips for Pinterest Success

- Do not add more than four images to one Pin.
- Use clear high-quality images for your Pins.
- Infographics work well on Pinterest.
- Create vertical pins to optimize for mobile devices.
- Add a short description to the Pin.
- Share, follow, and comment on high volume "repins"
- Make use of **Rich Pins**. Rich Pins allow you to add extra information to your page such as the product price, author name, location, etc.
- Use text overlays to add additional information about your Pins.
- Create separate boards for each of your products. Do not clump them all

together.
- Create a board for your customers asking them to post Pins of themselves using your product.
- Use **Shop the Look** pins to add product information, and direct visitors to your site.
- Use clear-text overlays on images to show more information about your product or service.
- Run cost-per-click ads to promote a pin. Note that you cannot add call-to-actions or buy buttons in your Pin.
- Do not post anything that is time-sensitive, e.g. text that says "Just in" because it will not be "Just in" in 5 years' time.

Reddit

Reddit is an online forum with over 330 million users. You need to subscribe to Subreddits, which are niche communities. The bigger the community, the more people you can reach.

Redditors hate self-promotion and excessive link sharing, regardless of whether you join a subreddit or not. Your posts can get up-voted or down-voted, depending on how many people rate them. Contribute to subreddits and share relevant content to market effectively as you will need to build a reputation and not just plug your own work.

Redditors are quick to comment if they feel you are violating the rules, which can result in a ban. Always check Subreddit rules before you post.

The one self-promotion that garners few complaints from Redditors (if you post to the relevant subreddit) is free stuff. If you have published a free eBook related to your product or business (and I strongly suggest you do) you can submit the link to free eBook Subreddits.

Reddit do offer paid advertising. However, the return on investment is not as good as other social media, paid advertising, platforms.

―――

Email Marketing

You should be able to run your email marketing campaigns from your CMS. Most shopping carts have an autoresponder to create your opt-in form. Also, MailChimp is the most popular platform for automating email campaigns. However, MailChimp is not free. You could also try Marketo, ConstantContact, and ActiveCampaign, or Salesforce Marketing Cloud if you are operating a business-to-business e-commerce site.

91% of people check their email daily. With a strong subject line, you have the potential to increase your conversions. In fact, email marketing has 3 times more conversions that social media marketing.

Use no more than 20 lines of text in your campaign, a call-to-action button and one graphic. Place all your important information at the top of the email so that it shows in the preview pane. Do not include videos that are more than 90 seconds long and add hyperlinks to your images. Do not use a lot of text, multiple columns or small fonts.

Send out emails once a week. Send them out too frequently, and your emails will be classed as spam.

More Email Best Practices:

- Segment your list of contacts to target specific customers, e.g. their purchase history or age.
- Set up autoresponder messages.
- Use the same email with different subject lines.
- Study your performance metrics, so that you can build on what is working by tracking your clicks, open, bounce and spam complaint rates.
- Emails should be mobile responsive.
- Pitch your business in no more than 20% of your posts.
- Test your content before sending out your campaign.
- Make use of seasonal/event email marketing opportunities.
- Avoid JavaScript and CSS elements because email providers will block these.
- Avoid spam trigger words.
- Avoid strange formats and symbols.
- Check your unsubscribe rates.

Lead Generation

Lead generation is centered around growing your business. Start with your key objective. This is to make sales.

Research has shown that customers are more likely to make a purchase from you after the 7th exposure. This does not mean that you should bombard potential or existing customers with lots of emails. You should follow-up on your leads with content showing what you have to offer and that offer should be of value: i.e. a discount, a giveaway, a resolution to a problem.

If you go onto an online store, leave it and later visit another site, you may start to see ads appearing from the website that you viewed earlier. This is because you are being retargeted with the 7th exposure rule in mind. See it enough and you may just hop back on to the site to make a purchase.

Practice retargeting and segmenting your audience based on their behavior on your site. You can get a better idea of why a person left your site by analyzing your web analytics.

You can capture leads in several ways. The most

obvious will be through your website. Other ways to capture leads include:

- Posting regular and relevant news or blog posts
- Facebook advertising that makes use of retargeting
- YouTube videos
- Webinars
- By engaging your customers on social media
- Publish an eBook (relevant to your business) with links to your site in the back page
- Google Advertising
- Running a giveaway or a competition
- Webinars/podcasts
- Posting on Instagram
- Collaborating with others in your industry. You can do this by networking at trade shows and joining small business initiatives. Check Eventbrite for these.

Lead Generation Tools

The tools listed below have lead capture pages, templates and the ability to conduct A/B split testing:

- LeadPages
- ClickFunnels
- Unbounce

These auto-responder services use automated marketing:

- AWeber
- Optinmonster
- ActiveCampaign
- Keap
- GetResponse
- MailChimp
- Marketo

Use Zendesk, if you want to centralise customer support. This will require customers to raise a ticket to a helpdesk if they have any enquiries. This may be something you want to consider if you are selling software or digital services.

——

Google Search Console

The Google Search Console provides useful information about your website. It tells you if your pages have been properly indexed, about any broken website links on your page, security issues, the number of visitors, search terms visitors used to find your site, and much more. This information is invaluable if you want to improve your SEO, improve your search engine ranking, determine product trends, and consumer demands.

Email notifications are automatically enabled. Google will email you if they are unable to crawl your site, if your account is hacked, or if you have violated their terms and conditions. They will advise you on how to resolve these issues.

I suggest that you check the Google Search Console once a week in case there are any issues you need to address.

- Sign into your Google account
- You will be asked to add your website URL, e.g. https://yourwebsitename.com
- Once you have done this, click on the ADD PROPERTY button

You will then be asked to verify your account. There are a few options available.

If you have a Google Analytics account set up for your domain, this will be the easiest option for account verification.

Google recommends HTML verification. Google will generate an HTML verification file which you can then upload to the File Manager on your virtual web hosting account.

Let us go through some of the more important features and how they can help you improve your website.

Enhancements
Mobile Usability
This will tell you about any issues with your site as displayed on mobile devices, e.g. small fonts.

Speed
Here you can view your website's speed on desktop and mobile devices.

Logos
This report will show any errors with your logo, if you have used structured mark-up. Your logo should be a minimum of 112px x 112px to meet display requirements.

Products
This report will show any rich results Google

displays in its SERPs for your site. Rich results can include rich snippets, rich cards and data highlights.

Rich snippets and rich cards increase visibility, but not your Google ranking. They can improve your click-through rate (CTR) because they provide visitors with more information about your site, making them more likely to click on it. And of course, an enticing image helps.

Rich Snippets

Rich snippets display the page URL, the page description, an image, and any reviews. Most content management systems provide Schema.org rich snippet extensions or plugins. Check with your developer or CMS provider. Ensure that you incorporate your main keyword in your rich snippet.

Rich Cards

This display can appear in Google's **Top Stories** and includes a horizontal scroll. They are good for displaying recipes, events and products.

Data Highlighting

If your website contains reviews or events, you may get a higher click through rate (CTR) if your data is highlighted even if your page has a low rank in the search engine. You can choose to tag various posts on your page. You can highlight and then label the important fields. To learn more, watch Google's short tutorial on the topic.

Sitelinks Searchbox
This is a company-specific search box that appears in Google SERPs and allows visitors to put in a search phrase directly in SERPs rather than on the company's website. It is popular with large e-commerce brands, like ASOS.

(AMP) Accelerated Mobile Pages
This allows you to display specification pages you want to display to mobile users. You will not rank higher if you have AMP-enabled pages on your website. However, these pages load faster and will show in Google's search engine results. This improves usability for mobile users. You should have a mobile-friendly version of your site in place prior to getting started with AMP.

An AMP-enabled page is indicated with a lightning bolt icon on mobile devices.

Performance
This gives you a quick analytical overview of your site's performance.

This will display your clicks, impressions, position, and the click through rate for each page on your website, the search terms users typed to find your website, their location, and the devices they used to access your website.

Links
Here you can view up to 10,000 backlinks and your most popular linked pages. It is important to check that you do not have any blacklisted or spam sites linking back to you.

Coverage
The Coverage report will display any crawl errors and any blocked resources. It will also show how many pages Google has indexed.

Crawl Errors
You can see how many times your page has been crawled; the more the better. This number should be going up. Check your sitemap. Note that if you have slow loading pages, the Google will take a long time to crawl your site.

- **404 errors** mean that the web page could not be found. You may have removed the web page or typed an incorrect URL.
- **500 Internal Server Errors** indicate that you have a problem with your internal server. These types of errors are difficult to trace. You will need to check the error log files on your virtual hosting account. Typical causes of 500 internal server errors can be:

o reduced disk space
o viruses
o incompatible plugins
o errors in permission settings.

Other error codes

- 301 is a permanent redirect
- 500 server page error.
- 302 redirect which is temporary for site

Changing an Existing URL with a 301 Redirect

You may decide to change a URL to optimize for search engines and/or because you have made significant changes to the content. If you fail to set a 301 redirect, you will not only have internal broken links on your site in the form of 404 error, but you are also in danger of losing valuable backlinks as no one wants a broken link on their site! Failing to set a redirect will negatively impact your SEO.

The great thing about WordPress and other good content management systems is that they automatically set the 301 redirects for you when you change the URLs. However, some content management systems will require you to install a "redirect" plugin.

Robots.txt for sites in development
If your website is still in development, you can add this HTML code to the **Header** section of the relevant page:

<META NAME="ROBOTS" CONTENT="INDEX, NOFOLLOW">

This will stop the page from showing in the search engine results. Check that you do not have a robots.txt file attached to the page, or this method will not work.

URL Inspection
Inspect a URL will tell you if Google has correctly indexed your URL. If it has not been indexed, you can request that Google re-indexes the page for desktop and/or mobile. You will want to do this if you have made changes to the web page, or URL, or you have pages that Google had previously flagged in your crawl error report but have since been corrected. It is a quick way to get pages that you have recently optimized showing in Google's search results. However, there is no guarantee that Google will re-index your pages via this method.

Sitemaps
A sitemap helps Google's site crawlers find all the pages on your website and can provide important metadata related to your website pages.

Your CMS should generate a sitemap listing all your pages or provide a plugin for you to do so.

If you do not have a sitemap, there are plenty of websites where you can generate one for free, if you have less than 500 pages on your website. Try XML Sitemaps. If you are using WordPress, you can install a free Google sitemap generator plugin or use the Yoast SEO plugin.

Security Issues and Manual Actions

This will detect cross-site malware and if your website has been hacked. Again, Google provides advice about how to resolve these issues. If Google has applied any penalties to your website(s), you will see them here.

Google Shopping Channel

Another great tool to promote your site is the Google product search tool, formerly known as Froogle. This will only work if you have added product images, SKUs and the part manufacturers' number to all your products. You need a data feed to upload your products to the shopping channel. Your shopping cart platform should have a plugin or extension to permit you to do this. If it does not, you will have to add them manually using a tab delimited text file.

This plug-in allows you to generate a product file from the default Google categories and add it to Google Shopping, which means more visibility for you and increased traffic.

You will need to open a Google Merchant Account and verify your website. You will need access to the code files to verify your account. You can also promote your products on Google Shopping through Google's paid advertising. This means that your products will show as images under the SPONSORED section on the page. You can create your Google Ads campaigns from your Google Merchant account.

Google Analytics

To effectively use Google Analytics, you will need to set your business goals, e.g. do you want to generate sales or drive awareness? Secondly, you will need to establish your key performance indicators (KPIs), i.e. what are you measuring your performance against? Perhaps, your KPIs are based on how many people sign-up for your newsletter and/or your resulting revenue. Next, decide if you want to set business targets based on your past performance or an industry benchmark.

Setting Up a Google Analytics Account

To view the number of unique visitors to your website and obtain other useful statistics about your website visitors, sign up for a Google Analytics (GA) account for your domain name.

You will be required to provide your website name, URL, and industry category.

Google Analytics will then generate a tracking ID, which you can add to your website. You should be able to add the GA tracking code to the designated text box field in your CMS.

Another method of adding tracking to your website is by using Google's Tag Manager. Your CMS should have plugins or extensions for tag management implementation.

Visit Google's Analytics Academy to learn more. They include a list of helpful video tutorials to get you started. Many of these video tutorials can also be found in the relevant sections of your GA dashboard.

Analyze the mobile and desktop versions of your site. To track your performance and obtain accurate reports:

- You will need to set up goals and e-commerce tracking in your Google Analytics account. Use goals for non-e-commerce tracking. You will require a developer or web administrator to set up e-commerce tracking on your website as this requires adding additional code to your web files. It is possible to do this in your CMS.
- In Property Settings, **Enable Demographics and Interest Reports** and **Enable Users Metric in Reporting**.
- For report accuracy, you will also need to set up **Filters** to ensure that neither yourself or your employees are included as web visitors in your reports. To do this, you will need to enter your IP address(s). To find your IP address, simply Google "What is my IP address?"
- Give the filter a name, e.g. "My IP

address"
- Select a predefined filter type: Exclude
- Select source and destination: Traffic from the IP Addresses
- Finally, select the expression "that are equal to".
- You will also need to check the "exclude all hits from known bots and spiders" in the **View Settings** tab as you only want to count visits from humans.

Site Search

You can find Site Search in Google Analytics **Behavior Report**.

You want to set this up as it will tell you what visitors are looking for on your site. This internal site search data, will help you identify product, service, and user requirements.

For example, if visitors are regularly searching for shipping and returns information, it may indicate that this information is not clearly displayed on your site.

Another example is if visitors are regularly searching for "blue silk scarves" on your site and you only stock them in red; you may want to think about adding blue silk scarves to your inventory.

How to Set up Site Search in Google Analytics

Find the search bar on your website. Do a search just as a customer would. In this example, we have searched for the word coats on our lovingclothes.com website.

Look at the URL in your web browser. You are only interested in the text that appears *after* the "?" and before the "=" sign. In this case, "s". This is known as a **query parameter**.

https://lovingclothes.com/?**s**=coats

Click on the Settings cog icon, in the lower left-hand corner, of your Google Analytics dashboard:

- Select **View Settings**
- Select **Site Search Settings**
- Turn <u>on</u> **Site search Tracking**
- Enter your query parameter, in this case, **"s"**
- Click **Save**

What are the Important Metrics for E-Commerce Businesses?

Bounce Rate

One of the most important metrics you need to measure is bounce rate. This is the number of visitors that leave your site without visiting any other web pages. You need to work on reducing your bounce rate. A bounce rate close to the 100% mark, on the homepage and/or product pages, is usually an indication of navigation and/or technical issues.

To reduce your bounce rate:

- Improve the user experience by creating quality content and visually-appealing images and videos.
- Ensure that you have included all vital product information, e.g. size options.
- Run some product price comparison checks. Your competitors may be offering the same products as you at a better price.
- Run a site maintenance check. A high bounce rate may be the result of a slow loading web page.

Note that while it is normal to have a high bounce rate on blog posts and pages that only display videos, you should not be experiencing a high bounce rate on a multi-category website.

E-Commerce Conversion Metrics
Cart abandonment rate
The **Checkout Behavior** in the e-commerce section will display your checkout abandonment rate.

Cart abandonment can be down to pricing. However, it can also be due to an issue with your checkout process or a technical issue. Ask yourself the following questions:

- Have I correctly configured my payment gateways?
- Is my checkout process too complicated or lengthy for my target customers?
- Have I added any extra charges at the checkout?
- Are my shipping times too long?
- Have I offered a guest/quick checkout option for buyers who do not wish to register for an account?

MailChimp

You can use email marketing platforms like MailChimp to create custom emails to handle shopping cart abandonment. An email is sent to the customer shortly after they have abandoned their cart encouraging them to return. You can download MailChimp's app into your store. It integrates with several shopping cart software applications such as Magento, Shopify, WooCommerce, and PrestaShop.

Product performance

By examining your product performance, you should be able to make business decisions, such as product pricing, what sort of discounts and promotions to offer, which products to cross-sell, which products to promote, and which to discontinue.

Most consumers will do their online shopping over the weekend. The most popular shopping day is Sunday. Therefore, you should carry out any web maintenance or product updates during the week, set up your ad campaigns, and add your bestselling products to your homepage.

Repeat customers
Analyze the customer journey through your sales funnel. What activities and interactions did it take to turn your visitors into customers?

Customer retention affects Customer Lifetime Value (CLV), which is the projected profit a customer will generate during their lifetime. To increase profits from your existing customers, draw up an engagement strategy plan. Take advantage of email marketing, and retargeting ad campaigns, to encourage past customers to return to your website. In addition, offer discounts and loyalty rewards.

Refunds and returns checklist
Some refunds and returns cannot be helped. However, you need to ensure that you have taken precautions to reduce your refunds and

returns. Consider the following:

- Product quality
- Shipping times
- Size/dimensions on product listing
- Pricing
- Concise refunds and returns policy
- Accurate product descriptions and product titles.
- Clear product images. The photos should reflect the actual products, so avoid excessive retouching.

Acquisition (how people found your website)

Once you have set up goals, you can monitor the effectiveness of your advertising campaigns and monitor user engagement on your social media platforms. The **All Traffic** report displays the source of traffic for your conversions, i.e. revenue.

By analyzing the acquisition channels and referrals, you can decide where to target your ad campaign spending. You should have calculated your average acquisition costs, or have an amount in mind that you want to spend on your ad campaigns.

You need to increase or reallocate your campaign spending on acquisition channels and referrals that generate the highest revenue. Use your best performing channels and referrals. These may not necessarily be the ones that drive the highest amount of traffic.

For example, you may find you get a lot of organic traffic (that is traffic from unpaid search results) but few of these visitors become customers. On the other hand, you may get less traffic from your Facebook page but more customers. You should therefore increase your market efforts on Facebook and improve your on-site optimization.

How to Use Google Data Studio to Create Reports

Despite its appearance, the Data Studio is relatively simple to use as Google can automatically populate the data for you. Rather than start with a blank report, I suggest you start with one of Google's templates, which you can customize with the data you want to track.

To create accurate reports for your data, you first need to set up **Goals** and e-commerce tracking which fall under the **Views** heading. This will make it easier to create your report in the studio. If you fail to set up Goals and e-commerce tracking, you can still create reports for all your web data.

Click on "All Web Site Data in the upper left-hand corner of your Google Analytics dashboard and select the blue Data Studio icon.

Click on the sample "Acme Marketing" template. Select the **Use Template** tab in the upper right-hand corner. Click the down arrow on the **Choose Data Source** and then click on the CREATE NEW DATA SOURCE link.

Click on the link and you will be taken to a list of **Connectors**. Select Google Analytics. Allow the connection and select your web domain to compile your reports.

.

_____

Advertising

Advertising is a way of communicating your message to your existing and potential customers. As a small business, you need to be able to connect with your audience in the right place and at the right time. To do this, you should know who your audience is and where to find them.

You should adopt a S.M.A.R.T approach to your advertising strategy. Ask yourself is your strategy:

- Specific?
- Measurable?
- Achievable?
- Realistic?
- Timely?

Specific

Your advertising strategy needs to be relevant to your customer and executed with an accurate and simple message.

You will have two objectives. The obvious one is to make money through sales, and the second is to build brand awareness. You need to let your customers know what makes you stand out from your competitors. What products and/or services do you have to offer that they do not?

You cannot afford to waste money. Conduct research first to identify your customers' needs and where they are located. You can conduct online surveys on platforms like Survey Monkey. You can also use Nielsen for insights data and global information.

Measurable

Your advertising campaign needs to be measurable. You should be able to track its progress, and be constantly testing, learning, and improving. You can use online tools, like Similar Web and moat.com, to research your competition.

Achievable

You need to be realistic about your advertising strategy. There is nothing wrong with being ambitious, but if you set the bar too high, you are bound to fail. Do you have the resources, time and budget to effectively execute your advertising campaign?

Realistic

You should know your budget, the total

available market for your niche, and your customer persona, i.e. the personality type of your potential customer. In addition, you will need to know what stage they are at in the sales funnel.

Focus on the customer experience and how you will connect with your customers. To begin with, concentrate your advertising efforts on owned media, e.g. your website, social media platforms, and reviews.

Timely

Execute your advertising message at the right time. It could be seasonal, trend or even economical-driven, and it may involve a series of related advertising messages over a given period of time. You will also need to think about the days and times your customers are looking to buy your products and services.

Types of advertising

- Digital, e.g. websites, email, social media, forums, eBooks
- Print, e.g. magazines, brochures, flyers
- Video, e.g. TV and online videos
- Events
- Retail, e.g. promotional material

Pay-Per-Click Advertising

Pay-per-click (PPC) campaigns are created so that you only pay when someone clicks on your ad. To attract the right visitors, you need to select the right keywords. Decide where and when you want your ads to show.

To get the most out of your PPC campaigns, write an ad campaign strategy and do your keyword research. Decide what you want to achieve and then the amount you want to spend.

Many Bing users are over 55. They have a smaller market share than Google. That being said, their PPC campaigns are cheaper. If you are interested in Bing ads you can visit their website for more information.

For now, I am going to discuss running ad campaigns on the Google platform. Use this in conjunction with at least one other social media platform such as Facebook or Instagram.

1. Set clear goals for your advertising campaign. Decide if you want to promote a category, a product, a service, or your blog.
2. If you are just launching your online business, direct traffic to your home page rather than a specific page on your

website.

3. Match the ad to your landing page and include at least one keyword and a call to action.

4. Run a test campaign. Try different ad formats. See what is working and then repeat it.

5. Do retargeting campaigns for visitors who came to your website but did not convert.

6. To avoid wasting money, it is important to regularly check your ad campaigns, and track your conversions to see how they are performing and adjust your bids accordingly. Increase bids on high performing keywords; decrease or remove bids on less effective keywords.

Google Ads – Tips for Managing Your Campaigns

• You may be raring to go with your ad campaign, but to avoid spending money on non-converting keywords, you must first compile your keyword strategy.

• If you are new to Google Ads, start with a budget of between $15.00 to $60.00. You could set a daily budget of $15.00, and then increase your bid on individual keywords.

• You need to make sure that your ads are relevant and the link takes the user to the correct landing page. Ads with a poor Quality Score* can result in your ads not showing on Google's search results.

- Although display ads are known to generate more clicks and less conversions, running both text and display ads alongside each other is the best way to optimize your conversions.
- If you are new to Google Ads, set a fixed daily budget and use the Maximize Clicks Bid strategy. Focus on one or two locations and one language to save money until you become more familiar with keyword optimization.
- Use the Keyword Search Planner, Keyword Diagnosis and the Opportunities feature to compile a list of your best keywords.
- Select a list of negative keywords to avoid paying for clicks on products that you do not sell.
- Set up separate Campaigns for display and text ads.
- Use Ad extensions.
- Write mobile-friendly ads to target people on mobile devices.
- Add a call-to-action.
- Use at least one keyword search term in your text ad.
- Use tools like AdSpike and AdStage to schedule, create and optimize your ad campaigns.
- Monitor your ads on the go with the

Google Ads app.
- If your keyword bids are not high enough to get you on the first page, increase your bid.
- To simplify tracking your conversions, link your Google Ads account to your Google Analytics account.
- Use brand keywords for repeat customers.
- Go for conversion relevant keywords and not popular search terms. For example, if you are selling a book about self-publishing. Avoid search terms like "kindle publishing" and "Amazon publishing". People searching for these terms are likely to be looking for information or products on Amazon's website.
- Pause keywords that are not performing.

*Ad Rank is where and when your ads will appear. This is determined by your bid amount and Quality Score. Quality Score is the expected click-through-rate (CTR), ad relevance and ad formats.

———

How to Generate Web Traffic

Once you have set up your Google Analytics account, you will no doubt find yourself checking the number of web visitors to your site. Many business owners base the success of their business on the number of visitors to their website and not their business objectives. Web traffic to your site must be relevant and drive your business objectives.

- Search Engine Optimization - applying SEO techniques that will get your site evaluated by search engines, and indexed, will increase your organic web traffic and thus your advertising spend.
- Buy a top-level domain, i.e. a .com or .net domain. These domains rank higher than second-level domain names like .tv or .biz.
- Add share buttons to your site to allow web visitors to share your content across the web.
- Participate in forums. Take the lead by starting a discussion on a topic for which you have existing content. Add a link to this content in your forum.
- Use influencers to promote your content and services. You can ask influencer bloggers to view your content. If they like it, they will share it.

- Add links to content in your site, in the centre of guest posts hosted, on high-quality sites.
- Promote giveaways in the form of contests. You can use platforms like Gleam or Reddit. The name of your prize should be your keyword.
- Do some A/B testing to discover which content drives the most traffic. You can create two variations of the same content to see which ranks higher.
- Create a content marketing strategy. Define your target audience and consider your key objectives: drive sales, sign-up for a newsletter. Post regularly.
- Use 4Shared.com to share files, e.g. videos, books, music, photos. See what others are sharing and upload a file of the same name.
- Use affiliate programs.
- Launch an email campaign and email promotions with discount coupons.
- Run PPC ads or Facebook ads.
- Create a Google Search Console account and request indexing of URLs.
- Do not add lots of duplicate content on your site
- Use YouTube to publish videos that relate to your business.
- Try AdBlade. They embed content-style ads on other sites in your niche. These ads will look like part of the advertising site, so visitors are more likely to click on

them.
- Create and publish your content on other platforms such as LinkedIn or eZine Articles.
- Write an evergreen blog post that will not become dated if it is read 10 years from now. Add a catchy headline that uses a long-tail keyword and a call-to-action. The article should be between 1000-2000 words long. Once posted, share it on social media.
- Sign up to the blogger-promotional exchange website, viralcontentbee.com. Link your social media accounts and get influencers to share your content.
- Check out ispionage.com. It will give you an advantage over your competitors by showing you the paid and free keywords they are using.
- Do not add lots of ads or external links to your site as search engines will rank it as spam and your search engine rankings will decline.

———

Website Maintenance

- Add new products regularly and share them via your smart buttons.
- Write regular blog posts.
- Send newsletters about any special offers, or events, to your email subscribers.
- Make full use of promotional banners for new products, special offers and announcements.
- Remember to add unique content. Do not copy and paste material from other websites.
- Regularly check your website for broken links that can hurt your search engine rankings. If you have written a blog, for example, and included a link to the product on your page that you have since deleted, remove it. You can use Google Search Console to check for these.
- Regularly update the front page of your website. This is your shop window. Display your new products, services and on-sale items.
- Check your website and social media data to improve on what is working and abandon, or modify what is not.

———

About the Author

Web developer and Google Certified Professional, S. K. Holder, has over ten years' experience in online retail, specifically in the dropshipping and affiliate marketing sectors.